My Prophet , Myself

My Prophet ﷺ, Myself

DANA NASS

rabata
Daybreak Press

© 2024 by Daybreak Press

All rights reserved. No part of this book may be reproduced or transmitted in any form or by any means, graphic, electronic or mechanical, including photocopying, recording, typing, or by any information storage retrieval system, without the permission of the publisher.

Daybreak Press
3533 Lexington Avenue North, Arden Hills, MN 55126
www.rabata.org/daybreakpress | daybreakpress@rabata.org

ISBN (print): 978-1-7368031-4-1
ISBN (ebook): 978-1-7368031-5-8
LCCN: 2025931076

Illustrations, cover art, & cover design: Zainab Arshad
Typesetting: Islam Farid | Islamfarid.net

Printed in the United States of America

Contents

1. Empathy 3
2. Trustworthiness 9
3. Self-Control 15
4. Contentment 21
5. Seeking Knowledge 25
6. Responsibility 29
7. Maintaining Ties of Kinship 35
8. Courage 41
9. Fairness 45
10. Generosity 51
11. Confidence 57
12. Grit 63
13. Honesty 69
14. Inclusivity 73
15. Loving for the Sake of Allah 79
16. Honoring Our Parents 83
17. Teamwork 89
18. Leadership 95
19. Kindness 101
20. Respect 109
21. Gratitude 113
Final Reflections 117
Glossary 118
Bibliography 125
Index 126
About the Author 128

To you, dear reader, who seeks to grow in
character and faith through these stories.

To my parents, who sparked my love
for the Prophet ﷺ early in my life.

To Anse Tamara, who never stopped believing in me.

To my husband, who has walked every
step of this journey with me.

Indeed, you stand exalted to a high and noble character. Quran 68:4

Assalamu alaikum! Welcome, scholars! I'll be your guide through *My Prophet ﷺ, Myself*—a journey into the character of **Prophet Muhammad ﷺ**. This book will help you develop some of the amazing traits he taught us. By learning these traits and following his example, we can spread kindness and light to everyone we meet inshallah.

In this book, we're going to explore twenty-one **characteristics** of the best teacher of all time ﷺ. You'll learn how our Prophet ﷺ **embodied** confidence, respect, trustworthiness, and many other traits. You'll learn how he taught us to be brave, honest, and grateful, even when it's hard. You'll learn how to include everyone, promote fairness, and be a good leader. And you'll learn how to live happily in this life and the next.

Along the way, there will be questions that will help you become more *self-aware*, or understand yourself better. Think of it like getting to know yourself on a deeper level. You'll recognize your strengths and pinpoint the areas that could use some work. Everyone has areas they need to work on, but—good news—we can develop good character traits over time. It's like building muscles at the gym—the more you work on them, the stronger they become. And trust me, it's not as hard as you think!

Let's begin! **Bismillah!**

1. Empathy

What Is Empathy?

Empathy means being aware of others' emotions and understanding what is bothering them. Having empathy means imagining yourself in someone else's shoes. We can develop empathy by being aware of how we act toward others, especially when they are going through difficult situations. Having empathy can also mean acting with kindness and being **considerate** of how others feel.

How Did the Prophet ﷺ Practice Empathy?

- Prophet Muhammad ﷺ never said words that would hurt others' feelings.
- He ﷺ listened to others when they shared their pain, without judging them. He showed them that he understood the feelings they were having.
- He ﷺ always showed support, offered to help, and never turned anyone down.
- He ﷺ would always accept gifts of food, and he ﷺ would never **criticize** the food he ate.
- He ﷺ played with his grandchildren, raced with his family members, and told jokes to make them feel better.

Empathy in Action

The Mother Bird

Prophet Muhammad ﷺ was kind and showed empathy to everyone, including animals. Once, some of his **companions** saw a bird's nest filled with baby chicks and decided to take the chicks out to hold them. When Prophet Muhammad ﷺ passed by, he saw the mother bird nervously flapping her wings and circling them in fear.

The Prophet ﷺ felt empathy for the scared mother bird and immediately asked his companions why they upset her. He told them to return her chicks to the nest. The companions quickly put the baby chicks back, and the mother bird became calm as soon as she saw her chicks were safe again.

Even though Prophet Muhammad ﷺ had a lot of responsibilities as he was spreading the message of Islam, he took the time to help the sad mother bird. He made sure her chicks were returned, so she could feel at ease.

The Crying Tree

When Prophet Muhammad ﷺ and his companions settled in Medina, the Prophet ﷺ bought a piece of land on which to build the new **masjid**. The Prophet ﷺ and his companions worked side by side to build the mosque. They used clay mixed with straw.

After several months of hard work, the masjid of the Prophet ﷺ was built. Muslims gathered together at the mosque to pray and listen to the Prophet ﷺ deliver his **khutbah**. The Prophet ﷺ would lean his back on a large tree that was inside the mosque while he gave his talks.

Over the years, more and more people embraced Islam. As the number of **attendees** at the masjid increased, people in the back rows were not able to see the Prophet ﷺ during his khutbahs. A woman from the Ansar had a **minbar** constructed that was three steps high, for the Prophet ﷺ to stand on while giving his khutbah. During his first speech on the new minbar, a crying sound echoed from within the mosque. The people soon realized that the whimpering was coming from the old tree. The Prophet ﷺ stopped his khutbah. He was aware of the tree's pain and hugged it until it quieted down. The tree was upset because it missed the Prophet ﷺ leaning on it while giving beautiful lectures about **Allah** ﷻ. The Prophet ﷺ showed empathy to all of Allah's creations.

Abu Umayr and His Little Bird

Prophet Muhammad ﷺ was visiting the family of Anas ibn Malik (*radi Allahu anhu*) in Medina and noticed that his little brother, Abu Umayr (*radi Allahu anhu*), was upset. He asked Abu Umayr's parents why their younger son was sad, and they told the Prophet ﷺ that his pet bird had died. Prophet Muhammad ﷺ understood the boy's heartache and wanted to comfort him. He ﷺ said a rhyme: "Oh Aba Umayr, what happened to **al-nughayr**?" (*Al-nughayr* means "the sparrow.")

No one's pain was ignored by the Prophet ﷺ. He cared about everyone's feelings, children's and adults', and showed this to Abu Umayr by asking him to share what had happened to his bird—and with a fun rhyme to cheer him up.

1. EMPATHY

Practical Application Questions

- Think of a time when someone showed empathy to you while you were going through a difficult time. How did that feel? List the positive feelings you felt.
- List ways you can show empathy to your friends, parents, family, and neighbors.
- Describe the characteristics you can see in a person who has empathy.

One of the ways Prophet Muhammad ﷺ showed empathy was by never criticizing the food he ate. How is this a type of empathy? *Hint: How would someone feel if you criticized the food they cooked?*

2. Trustworthiness

What Is Trustworthiness?

Trustworthiness means keeping your promises. A trustworthy person does what she says she will do. We are trustworthy in our actions when we act truthfully without tricking or hurting others. Acting trustworthy means doing the right thing, even when no one is looking. We can make sure to always be trustworthy by monitoring ourselves and remembering that Allah ﷻ is watching over us.

How Did the Prophet ﷺ Practice Trustworthiness?

- Prophet Muhammad's nickname before Islam was **al-Sadiq, al-Amin** (the Honest, the Trustworthy).
- The Meccans trusted him ﷺ with their secrets, valuable items, and money.
- When Prophet Muhammad ﷺ made a promise, he always kept his word and did what he said, no matter what happened or how long it took.
- Prophet Muhammad ﷺ always chose to do the right thing, even when it was difficult or scary.
- He ﷺ was always loyal to others and never betrayed people's trust.

Trustworthiness in Action

A Blessed Caravan

Khadija bint Khuwaylid (*radi Allahu anha*) was one of the **noblewomen** of Mecca. She was famous for her kindness, generosity, and great wealth. She was also a very successful businesswoman.

At that time, Mecca was the center of the trading route from Yemen to Syria. Trading **caravans** traveling along the route would stop in Mecca to rest and sell their goods. Khadija would send trading caravans with goods to sell in Yemen and Syria.

When Khadija wanted to send a caravan to Syria, she needed to hire someone honest to lead it because it would be full of precious goods. She heard about a young man who was known for being honest and trustworthy. His name was Muhammad! Prophet Muhammad ﷺ was twenty-five years old at the time and had some experience from traveling with his uncle's caravan. He accepted the job and led the huge caravan to Syria. Khadija sent her assistant Maysara to help him on the trip. Prophet Muhammad ﷺ was able to sell the goods and earn a great **profit** for Khadija.

When the caravan returned to Mecca, Prophet Muhammad ﷺ went straight to Khadija's house. He gave her all of the special goods that he had purchased and the money he had made. Khadija was amazed—it was double the amount of money that previous caravans had made!

When she asked Maysara about the trip, he said he was impressed by the Prophet's character and honesty. "I have never met anyone like him!" This proved that young Muhammad was indeed trustworthy, honest, and blessed.

The Black Stone Dispute

When Prophet Muhammad ﷺ was thirty-five years old, a great flood hit Mecca and damaged the **Kaaba**. The leaders of Mecca came together to rebuild the Kaaba. They divided themselves into four groups based on their **lineage**, and each group's leader participated in the process. Banu Abd Manaf, the tribe Prophet Muhammad ﷺ belonged to, was the most respected.

Everything was going smoothly until they came to the Black Stone. The leaders started fighting about who would get the honor of placing the Black Stone into its corner in the Kaaba. Even before Islam, people knew how special the Black Stone was. Each tribe's leader believed his tribe deserved the honor of putting it back into its place. They argued for five long days, until Mecca was on the **brink** of war. Finally, one man told them to stop fighting and suggested a new plan—whoever entered the gate of the Kaaba next would decide who got to place the Black Stone. The leaders accepted.

Just then, Prophet Muhammad ﷺ entered the gate. Everyone was so happy to see him, even those who were not from his tribe. They said, "Muhammad is the Honest and the Trustworthy! We won't find a better judge than him." They knew he would not favor his own tribe to receive this honor. Everyone trusted that the Prophet ﷺ would make a fair and honest decision.

After Prophet Muhammad ﷺ listened to their problem, he came up with a great idea. He asked them to bring a piece of cloth, lay it on the ground, then lift the Black Stone together and place it in the middle of the cloth. Then the leader of each tribe carried one side of the cloth toward the Kaaba. Then Prophet Muhammad ﷺ lifted the Black Stone into its place. He ﷺ saved Mecca from a huge fight, and everyone was happy that their tribe received the honor of carrying the Black Stone.

What could have happened if Prophet Muhammad ﷺ hadn't solved the dispute over the Black Stone?

The Trustworthy One

When Prophet Muhammad ﷺ declared the message of Islam in Mecca, the people of **Quraysh** were angry. They wanted everyone to continue worshipping their false gods and **idols**. Some feared what other people would think of them if they worshipped one God. Others made a lot of money creating and selling idols; if people stopped worshipping them, they would lose their businesses.

The people of Quraysh planned to stop the Prophet ﷺ from spreading the message of Islam by hurting the Muslims. They called them names and were very **cruel** to them. But no matter what they did, the Muslims would not go back to worshipping idols. The people of Quraysh soon became furious, and they held a meeting to come up with a new plan. By the end of the meeting, they had decided to kill the Prophet ﷺ in order to stop the message of Islam from spreading. The Quraysh thought they had a smart plan: They selected a leader from each tribe and planned to attack the Prophet ﷺ when he left his house for **Fajr** (dawn) prayer.

Allah ﷻ, the All-Hearing and All-Knowing, knew about their evil plan. He informed the Prophet ﷺ about their plot and commanded him to leave for Medina secretly, along with his beloved companion Abu Bakr al-Siddiq (*radi Allahu anhu*).

Prophet Muhammad ﷺ went in secret to Abu Bakr's house to tell him of the new plan. Abu Bakr was extremely happy to be chosen to accompany the Prophet ﷺ, despite the difficult situation. He loved the Prophet ﷺ so much, and he wanted to make sure he ﷺ arrived safely in Medina.

As they were putting together a plan to escape without anyone noticing, Prophet Muhammad ﷺ remembered **al-amanat** (the trusts) he had that belonged to the people of Quraysh. At that time, there weren't banks to store people's money or protect their valuable items. Since the people of Mecca knew their money would be safe with the Prophet ﷺ, they would often leave it with him ﷺ when they had to travel. He would keep it safe until they came back.

Even though the people of Quraysh were plotting to kill Prophet Muhammad ﷺ, he did not take any of their money or **possessions**. Instead, he left them with his cousin, Ali ibn Abi Talib (*radi Allahu anhu*), whom he ﷺ asked to stay behind and return the trusts to their owners. Allah ﷻ protected Prophet Muhammad ﷺ from the people of Quraysh, and he arrived safely in Medina. Ali (*radi Allahu anhu*) was also safe and helped prove that Prophet Muhammad ﷺ was always the Honest, the Trustworthy.

Practical Application Questions

- Think of a time when you chose to be trustworthy, even though it was difficult. What happened? How did that make you feel?
- List ways you can practice trustworthiness at school.
- Describe the characteristics you can see in a trustworthy person.

3. Self-Control

What Is Self-Control?

Self-control means managing your emotions, actions, and words. Having self-control means being able to stop and think before reacting to something negative. A person with self-control can manage their feelings, even when they become angry or upset. When you practice self-control, you can focus on your goals and not let failure or difficulties stop you. You will have more willpower, and it will be easier to avoid **temptations**.

How Did Prophet Muhammad ﷺ Practice Self-Control?

- Prophet Muhammad ﷺ had great self-control. It helped him spread the message of Islam even when things were difficult.
- Prophet Muhammad ﷺ was a great listener. He did not interrupt people when they were speaking, and he always used a calm voice.
- He ﷺ consistently followed the rules.
- Even though he ﷺ faced many challenges in his life, he did not get frustrated and never gave up on spreading the message of Islam.
- Sometimes people would speak rudely to the Prophet ﷺ or try to annoy him, but he always controlled his emotions and his words.

Self-Control in Action

"Beware of That Man!"

One day, as Prophet Muhammad ﷺ was running errands in the outskirts of Mecca, he saw an elderly lady carrying heavy bags. Prophet Muhammad ﷺ offered to help her. He always loved helping those around him. The old lady was happy he offered to carry the bags for her—it was still a long way to Mecca and the bags were really heavy. He carried her bags and walked with her toward Mecca.

The lady was very impressed with the Prophet's manners. She decided to warn him about a man she had heard about in Mecca. He was calling everyone to worship one God and telling them to stop worshipping idols. She had heard horrible things about that man called Muhammad.

"Beware of that man named Muhammad! He is a magician and an evil person. He is tricking people into leaving their gods to worship only one God. That man is a liar and is splitting the community in Mecca. *You seem to be a good person, so do not let this man* **deceive** *you!*"

Even though the lady was describing Prophet Muhammad ﷺ with hurtful words and accusing him of being a liar and a magician, Prophet Muhammad ﷺ remained silent. He listened to her all the way to Mecca and did not get angry or interrupt her to defend himself. He continued to carry her bags, despite her hurtful words.

Prophet Muhammad ﷺ controlled his feelings the whole time and remained calm and kind. Once they arrived at her house, he put down her bags.

"What was your name?" she asked before leaving.

"I am Muhammad!" Prophet Muhammad ﷺ replied.

The old lady was shocked! She realized he was the man she had been talking about. "I was talking about you all this time, and you did not get angry with me! I do not believe anything people are saying about you now. I believe you truly are the Messenger of Allah ﷻ. I bear witness that there is no god except Allah, and I bear witness that Muhammad is the Messenger of Allah." She embraced Islam on the spot.

3. SELF-CONTROL

أَشْهَدُ أَنْ لَا إِلَهَ إِلَّا اللَّهُ وَأَشْهَدُ أَنَّ مُحَمَّدًا رَسُولُ اللَّهِ

Ashhadu an la ilaha illallah wa ashhadu anna Muhammadan Rasullullah!

Prophet Muhammad's amazing self-control led to her embracing Islam. He did not have to say anything—his beautiful actions convinced her!

Quraysh's Offer

As we discussed in Chapter 2, when Prophet Muhammad ﷺ declared the message of Islam, the people of Quraysh were angry. They wanted people to continue worshipping idols. They worried about what other tribes in the Arabian Peninsula would say about them. Some worried that if people stopped worshipping idols, their businesses would fail because many Meccans made idols and sold them during **Hajj (pilgrimage)**. The people of Quraysh did everything they could think of to stop the Prophet ﷺ from preaching about Islam. They called him a "magician" and a "liar" in public, threw trash at his house, and made fun of him ﷺ and the believers.

The leaders of Mecca came up with a new plan to stop the Prophet ﷺ from teaching about Islam. They made an offer to the Prophet's uncle, Abu Talib. One of them said, "If your nephew, Muhammad, is looking for **fame**, we can make him into a powerful leader. If he is looking for wealth, we can give him a lot of gold and beautiful treasures. All that we need from him is to stop calling people to Islam."

Abu Talib loved Prophet Muhammad ﷺ and was his biggest protector. Because Abu Talib was a leader of Mecca, no one was able to hurt the Prophet ﷺ directly. Abu Talib was getting older, though, and he worried about what would happen to the Prophet ﷺ after he passed away. *How will the leaders of Mecca treat my nephew after I pass?* he wondered.

Abu Talib asked the Prophet ﷺ to meet with him. When he arrived at his uncle's house, Abu Talib looked at him with love and said, "Come sit next to me, my dear nephew. I want to share Quraysh's offer with you, and I hope you will accept it. I worry about what will happen to you after I pass away. Who will protect you from the harm of the Quraysh?"

Because he loved the Prophet ﷺ, and was worried about him, Abu Talib explained the offer to him and tried to convince him to stop teaching about Islam.

Prophet Muhammad ﷺ used his excellent self-control. He listened to Abu Talib respectfully and did not get angry. He ﷺ said: "Oh my uncle, even if they put the sun in my right hand and moon in my left, I will not give up this mission [of spreading God's word] until I die."

Prophet Muhammad ﷺ controlled his emotions and calmly declined the offer. He resisted the temptation of having power in Mecca. He did not let their offers of fame and money stop him from reaching his goal of spreading the message of Islam.

Do Not Get Angry

Once, one of the companions came to Prophet Muhammad ﷺ and said, "Please give me a piece of advice."

Prophet Muhammad ﷺ said: "Do not get angry."

The man asked the Prophet ﷺ for more advice, and the Prophet ﷺ again answered: "Do not get angry."

The man asked again, and the Prophet ﷺ answered: "Do not get angry."

Even though this might sound like simple advice, Prophet Muhammad ﷺ recognized the importance of controlling our anger. If we control our emotions and our anger, we can control everything else. When we let our emotions take control, everything else goes out of control. It becomes hard to think clearly.

A person who controls their anger is powerful. Prophet Muhammad ﷺ said: "The powerful person is not the one who can wrestle, but the powerful person is the one who can control themself at the time of anger."

Next time you're talking with someone, remember the Prophet ﷺ and focus on listening to what they're saying to you. Remind yourself not to interrupt them. How did the other person feel when you listened so well? How did you feel when you didn't interrupt? This is a form of self-control!

3. SELF-CONTROL

What does it mean to be powerful according to Prophet Muhammad's advice?

Practical Application Questions

- Think of a time when you used self-control before acting or speaking. What happened? How did controlling yourself help you?
- List ways you can practice self-control at school.
- Describe the characteristics you can see in a person with self-control.

4. Contentment

What Is Contentment?

Being content means being satisfied with what you already have without wanting newer, bigger, or better things. Having contentment requires self-control and an effort to appreciate what we have. We have to understand that happiness comes from the heart—not the things we own. If we are always focused on getting new things, we won't be grateful for the blessings we have all around us, and we won't feel content.

Prophet Muhammad ﷺ taught us the secret necessary to finding happiness in this life: being content with what Allah ﷻ has chosen for us! Because of His ﷻ love for us, Allah ﷻ chooses what's best for us in this life and the next.

How Did the Prophet ﷺ Practice Contentment?

- Prophet Muhammad ﷺ never complained about the difficulties in his life and was happy with everything that Allah ﷻ chose for him.
- He ﷺ taught us not to look at others' wealth, but to look at people who have less than we do and to be grateful for what we have.
- Prophet Muhammad ﷺ encouraged his companions to focus on true happiness, which comes from having a content heart and not from getting more stuff.
- He ﷺ taught us that having contentment protects us from becoming greedy.
- Prophet Muhammad ﷺ told us that a true believer wants good things for his Muslim brothers and sisters, just like he wants good things for himself.

Contentment in Action

Manners Matter

Prophet Muhammad ﷺ was the best of humankind. He embodied Islamic manners in each part of his life and taught us how to act as Muslims. He used every opportunity to teach his companions **adab**, or Islamic manners.

One day, a young boy, Umar ibn Abi Salama (*radi Allahu anhu*), was eating next to the Prophet ﷺ. It was part of their culture to share food from the one large platter instead of everyone having their own plate. Umar was grabbing food from all over the platter, reaching his arm in front of other people.

Upon seeing this, the Prophet ﷺ taught him proper *adab*: "Dear child, mention Allah's name, eat with your right hand, and eat from what is in front of you."

This teaching has been practiced by Muslim children for the past 1,400 years. In this **hadith**, Prophet Muhammad ﷺ teaches us not to be greedy. Rather than reaching for the good stuff we may want that's far away from us, we should eat what's in front of us. It's an opportunity to be content with whatever food we have and to be considerate of others.

A Lesson in Charity

Ali ibn Abi Talib (*radhi Allahu anhu*) and his wife Fatima (*radi Allahu anha*), the daughter of Prophet Muhammad ﷺ, decided to fast for three days with their two sons, Hasan and Husayn (*radi Allahu anhuma*). That evening, Ali was able to bring home enough food for iftar. When it was almost time to break their fast, a poor man knocked at their door asking for food. Ali gave him the food he had brought home—the only food they had in the house—without thinking twice. They were content with having only water for their dinner, and they went to sleep feeling hungry.

The following day they fasted again, and just like the previous day, Ali was able to bring home just enough food for their iftar that night. When it was time for Maghrib, an orphan knocked at their door asking for food. They gave him the only food they had and went to sleep after drinking some water.

On the third day, while they were getting ready for iftar, a man knocked at their door asking for food, and again, they gave away everything they had to eat. Ali, Fatima, Hasan, and Husayn went to sleep without eating for the third day in a row. They loved for their brothers what they loved for themselves. Even though they were hungry, they were content with having only water. They happily gave away all their food for the sake of Allah ﷻ.

$$وَيُطْعِمُونَ ٱلطَّعَامَ عَلَىٰ حُبِّهِۦ مِسْكِينًا وَيَتِيمًا وَأَسِيرًا ۝$$

$$إِنَّمَا نُطْعِمُكُمْ لِوَجْهِ ٱللَّهِ لَا نُرِيدُ مِنكُمْ جَزَآءً وَلَا شُكُورًا ۝$$

They give food to the poor, the orphan, and the captive, though they love it themselves, saying, "We feed you for the sake of God alone: We seek neither recompense nor thanks from you." Quran 76:8–9

For Richer or Poorer

Mus'ab ibn Umayr (*radi Allahu anhu*) was a handsome young man in Mecca. He was raised in an extremely wealthy family and was the only son of his mother, Khunnas. From the time he was a little child, she dressed him in special clothes made from the best silk. He also wore the most expensive perfume. When he passed by a place, people could smell his perfume for days after. Whatever Mus'ab wore would later become **trendy** in Mecca—everyone wanted to be just like him.

Eventually, Mus'ab heard about the message of Islam. He knew how honest and trustworthy Prophet Muhammad ﷺ was, so he decided to speak to him. He went to Dar al-Arqam and heard the Prophet ﷺ speaking to his companions about **Janna** (Paradise) and the Day of Judgment. When Prophet Muhammad ﷺ finished speaking, Mus'ab embraced Islam and said his **shahada** (declaration of faith) on the spot. Prophet Muhammad ﷺ was overjoyed to see him accept Islam, but he ﷺ asked Mus'ab to keep his faith a secret because Islam had not been announced publicly yet.

Mus'ab learned everything he could about his new religion and became a regular attendee at Dar al-Arqam. He would go there secretly in the dark to make sure no one saw him. But one day, someone saw Mus'ab praying near the Kaaba and told his mother, Khunnas. When she asked him about it, he admitted that he was a Muslim and invited her to embrace Islam, but she would not. She tried to convince him to leave Islam, but nothing she said would change his mind. Allah ﷻ had guided him.

Khunnas locked Mus'ab up in their house and ordered her men to watch him. She took away all his wealth and fancy clothes. He patiently waited for his mother to release him, reciting verses of the Quran he had learned from the Prophet ﷺ in his beautiful voice.

While he was still locked in his house, Mus'ab heard that the Prophet ﷺ had allowed some Muslims to leave Mecca for Abyssinia. He managed to escape and join them with only the clothes on his back. Although he was once the most well-dressed and popular young man in Mecca, he ran from his city with no money and no family. He stayed with the Muslims in Abyssinia for many years. When he came back to Mecca, Mus'ab gently tried to convince his mother to accept Islam, but she still insisted that he leave Islam. She threatened to chain him up again and disown him entirely.

Prophet Muhammad ﷺ loved Mus'ab dearly and trusted him greatly. He ﷺ asked Mus'ab to move to Yathrib (Medina) to teach the people, especially the new Muslims there, about Islam. Mus'ab represented Islam with his beautiful manners, contentment, and **sincere** love for Allah ﷻ and the Prophet ﷺ. Many people there became Muslim under his guidance during the first year of his stay.

One day, the Prophet ﷺ noticed that the clothes Mus'ab wore were made of rough sackcloth. He remembered how Mus'ab used to dress in the best clothes in Mecca. When Prophet Muhammad ﷺ saw the sores on Mus'ab's skin from the rough material, he cried and made *dua* (a prayer) for him. Mus'ab never looked back at his **luxurious** life, because his faith gave him contentment. He was content with his love for Allah ﷻ.

How did Mus'ab's appearance change after he became a Muslim? Why do you think he made that change?

Practical Application Questions

- Think of a time when you were excited to get a new game for Eid but got bored after beating all of the levels. Did you want to get a newer game soon after? How does being satisfied with what we have, without wanting something newer or better, make us happier?
- List ways social media can affect our contentment with what Allah ﷻ has provided us.
- Describe the characteristics you can see in a content person.

5. Seeking Knowledge

What Does It Mean to Seek Knowledge?

We seek knowledge when we are **eager** to learn new things. When you seek knowledge, you understand more and more and become **empowered**. The first word revealed to our beloved Prophet ﷺ in the Quran was the word *iqra,* which means "read"—to seek knowledge! This shows us the great importance of seeking knowledge and learning in Islam.

How Did the Prophet ﷺ Seek Knowledge?

- Prophet Muhammad ﷺ understood the importance of knowledge, even though that was an uncommon view at his time.
- He ﷺ promised those who seek knowledge a great reward and a special place in Janna.
- Prophet Muhammad ﷺ wanted us to be lifelong learners.
- Prophet Muhammad ﷺ always found ways to teach his companions and challenged them to expand their knowledge. He asked Zayd ibn Thabit (*radi Allahu anhu*) to learn **Hebrew** in just two weeks so he could be the Prophet's interpreter!

Seeking Knowledge in Action

The First Islamic School

During the early days of Islam, there were around twenty believers. They had embraced Islam secretly to avoid harm from the Quraysh. The Muslims gathered with the Prophet ﷺ at the house of a man named al-Arqam ibn Abi al-Arqam (*radi Allahu anhu*). He was from the noblemen of Quraysh and was one of the first ten people to embrace Islam. Prophet Muhammad ﷺ trusted him completely.

Prophet Muhammad ﷺ understood the importance of seeking knowledge. He wanted new believers to love Allah and learn how to make their hearts pure. The Muslims had to be careful, though, because the leaders of Mecca tried to hurt anyone who became a Muslim. So Prophet Muhammad ﷺ chose al-Arqam's house as a meeting place. It was in the center of Mecca, right behind the hill of al-Safa, and was busy with crowds coming and going around the Kaaba. No one would suspect anything about the gatherings that took place there, especially since al-Arqam was just a teenager and had not announced his Islam.

In this blessed house, the companions gathered with the Prophet ﷺ and learned their religion from him. This was the first madrasa, or Islamic school. Many people embraced Islam there, and some of the Quran was revealed to the Prophet ﷺ in that house. For many years, Islamic knowledge was sought and taught at Dar al-Arqam as the Prophet ﷺ created a special community of Muslims. Here, Prophet Muhammad ﷺ was able to nurture the future leaders of the **ummah**.

Why was it important for new Muslims to learn from Prophet Muhammad ﷺ? Why do you think Dar al-Arqam was considered the first Islamic school?

Knowledge Is Valuable!

Two years after the migration to Medina, Muslims won their first victory over the people of Mecca in the Battle of Badr. Many Meccans had been captured by the Muslims during the battle. These captives were the same people who tried to kill the Muslims when they were in Mecca. However, Prophet Muhammad ﷺ chose to forgive them. He set a ransom for them based on their wealth. Whoever paid the ransom was set free and was allowed to go back to Mecca.

Those who did not have any money could gain their freedom by giving something valuable to the Muslims. What could be more valuable than money, though? Knowledge! Prophet Muhammad ﷺ recognized the value of knowledge. He considered it a type of wealth and wanted the companions to learn as much as possible.

Reading and writing were not common at that time, but Prophet Muhammad ﷺ wanted to empower his companions with knowledge. He decided that each prisoner who taught ten Muslims how to read and write would be set free. This brilliant idea of the Prophet's helped **dozens** of Muslims learn to read and write. This is one way Prophet Muhammad ﷺ showed us the importance of seeking knowledge anytime we can.

Why didn't Prophet Muhammad ﷺ make every captive pay a lot of money to be set free?

A Legacy of Learning

Aisha (*radi Allahu anha*) was the daughter of Abu Bakr (*radi Allahu anhu*), Prophet Muhammad's ﷺ closest companion, and one of the first believers. She was brought up in a household of knowledge. Abu Bakr was knowledgeable about Arab lineage and history. Aisha married the Prophet ﷺ after he migrated to Medina and lived with him until he passed away.

Aisha gained a lot of knowledge from the Prophet ﷺ and narrated more than 2,200 hadiths. She lived for more than fifty years after the Prophet ﷺ passed away and became a source of Islamic knowledge for Muslims. Thanks to his ﷺ life of teaching and her intelligence, memory, and faith, we have so many valuable hadiths from the Prophet ﷺ that we would not have had otherwise.

Aisha's unique personality traits, like courage and self-confidence, along with her knowledge, made her shine as a noble scholar. Her nephew, Urwa ibn al-Zubayr (*radi Allahu anhu*), mentioned that he had never met anyone as knowledgeable as Aisha. He said, "She was the most scholarly person of her time in the Quran, **fiqh**, poetry, Arabian history, and **genealogy**."

Aisha was a passionate teacher, and both men and women would attend her classes. She was dedicated to passing on her knowledge to Muslims, and proved herself to be a true student of the Prophet ﷺ.

Practical Application Questions

- Think of a time when you learned a new skill that helped you solve a problem easily. What happened? How did it make you feel?
- List ways to show respect to a teacher while seeking knowledge.
- Describe the characteristics you can see in a knowledgeable person.

6. Responsibility

What Is Responsibility?

Responsibility means doing the things you are required or expected to do. Being responsible means knowing what you need to do and sticking to it, even if no one is supervising you. When you take responsibility, you take ownership of your actions and decisions by making good choices. Accepting responsibility means you are accepting the consequences of your decisions and actions.

How Did the Prophet ﷺ Practice Responsibility?

- Prophet Muhammad ﷺ practiced responsibility by always doing what he said he would do.
- He ﷺ took on the responsibility of caring for all Muslims. He made sure they learned their *deen* (faith) and did everything he could to keep them safe.
- Prophet Muhammad ﷺ accepted the consequences of his decisions and did not blame others for his actions.
- The Prophet's main responsibility was spreading the message of Islam, and he always did his best—without making any excuses.

Responsibility in Action

Spreading the Light

One night in the month of Ramadan, Angel **Jibril (Gabriel)** (*alayhi al-salam*) visited Prophet Muhammad ﷺ in the cave of Hira and revealed the first verses of the Quran.

$$\text{اقْرَأْ بِاسْمِ رَبِّكَ الَّذِي خَلَقَ ۝ خَلَقَ الْإِنْسَانَ مِنْ عَلَقٍ ۝}$$
$$\text{اقْرَأْ وَرَبُّكَ الْأَكْرَمُ ۝ الَّذِي عَلَّمَ بِالْقَلَمِ ۝ عَلَّمَ الْإِنْسَانَ مَا لَمْ يَعْلَمْ ۝}$$

Read! In the name of your Lord who created: He created humans from a clinging form. Read! Your Lord is the Most Bountiful One who taught by the pen, who taught humanity what they did not know. Quran 96:1–5

Prophet Muhammad ﷺ wasn't sure that what had happened was real and, terrified, he ran back home. He told his wife Khadija (*radi Allahu anha*) the story and said: "I am scared for myself!"

Khadija replied, "Allah ﷻ will never disgrace you because you always do good."

The next day Khadija took the Prophet ﷺ to her cousin, Waraqa ibn Nawfal, a wise man who was knowledgeable about the scriptures of **Judaism** and other holy books. When Prophet Muhammad ﷺ explained what had happened, Waraqa excitedly said, "This is the same angel and keeper of secrets that came down to Musa [Moses]! How I wish I was still a young man, so I could support you when your nation **expels** you."

Prophet Muhammad ﷺ was shocked and asked: "Will my nation expel me?"

Waraqa replied, "Yes. Never has any prophet been sent except that his people expelled him."

A few days later, Waraqa passed away. From that day, Prophet Muhammad ﷺ recognized the important responsibility given to him. Even though he realized how difficult this path would be, he took full responsibility for the *da'wa* (inviting people to Islam) until the last day of his blessed life. He did not waste any opportunity to teach people about the oneness of Allah ﷻ. Even when people were rude to him or hurt him, he continued to find ways to spread the message of Islam.

No matter what the people of Mecca did to the Muslims, Prophet Muhammad ﷺ continued his duty to spread Islam throughout Mecca for thirteen years. When Allah ﷻ gave His permission, Prophet Muhammad and the Muslims migrated to Medina, where he ﷺ continued his responsibility of spreading the message of Islam. He taught people about Islam for ten more years there until he passed away. After the Prophet ﷺ passed away, his companions continued his work and spread Islam all the way to the borders of China.

6. RESPONSIBILITY

How did Waraqa's knowledge help Prophet Muhammad ﷺ prepare for his mission of *da'wa*?

A New Land

Prophet Muhammad ﷺ focused on spreading the message of Islam and taking care of the Muslims. When he announced the message of Islam, the leaders of Mecca tried to hurt anyone who followed him. But no matter what they did, the Muslims would not go back to worshipping idols. They knew they were on the right path. Five years after Prophet Muhammad ﷺ began his *da'wa*, however, things became **unbearable** for some of the Muslims.

Prophet Muhammad ﷺ was responsible for their safety and wanted to help them practice their religion without being harmed. He made a lot of *dua* and asked Allah ﷻ for help.

He considered migration to a new land. If the Muslims left Mecca, they would be far away from the cruelty of the Quraysh, but he had to make sure they would be safe and happy. He heard of a place in Africa that the Quraysh used to trade with called Abyssinia. Abyssinia was ruled by **al-Najashi**, a Christian king who was known for his justice. He let everyone in his land practice their religion freely.

The people of Abyssinia were Christians who worshipped God; they did not worship idols. They understood what a prophet was and believed in Prophet Isa (Jesus) (*alayhi al-salam*). Their religion was closer to Islam than the religion of the people of Mecca, who worshipped idols.

The next time the Prophet ﷺ met with his companions, he shared this idea of migrating to Abyssinia, where they could practice their faith freely. Abyssinia was outside of the Arabian Peninsula, so the Quraysh would have no power over the people who migrated. It was also close to Mecca—only a two- or three-day journey away.

Eleven men and four women companions set out from Mecca for Abyssinia, leaving all of their belongings behind. Among them was Uthman ibn Affan and his wife Ruqayya, the daughter of the Prophet ﷺ (*radi Allahu anhuma*). They made their way to the seaside, boarded a ship, and sailed to Abyssinia. Al-Najashi welcomed them and protected them. When the Quraysh asked him to expel the Muslims from his land, he refused and said, "I will never let down the people who sought my protection."

Those fifteen companions remained in Abyssinia for fourteen years until the Prophet ﷺ sent a letter to one of them—his cousin, Ja'far ibn Abi Talib (*radi Allahu anhu*)—instructing them to come back. Prophet Muhammad ﷺ took his responsibility of caring for the Muslims seriously and made a good choice by sending those fifteen to Abyssinia. They lived there happily and were able to practice their religion freely.

Preserving the Quran

The Holy Quran was first revealed to Prophet Muhammad ﷺ in the cave of Hira by the Angel Jibril (*alayhi al-salam*) in Ramadan, during the year 610 CE. It is the only holy book that has been **preserved** in its original form—with no changes at all—just as it was revealed. Allah ﷻ promised in the Quran 1,400 years ago that this book would be preserved forever, and by Allah's will, it has been!

The Quran was revealed to Prophet Muhammad ﷺ over a span of twenty-three years. The companions of the Prophet ﷺ memorized the

Quran by heart as it was revealed. Some companions wrote verses of the Quran on leather or different materials. They took on the responsibility of preserving the Quran even after Prophet Muhammad ﷺ passed away.

During the *khilafa* of Abu Bakr (*radi Allahu anhu*), seventy **huffaz** (people who had memorized the entire Quran) were killed in the Battle of Yamama. Umar ibn al-Khattab (*radi Allahu anhu*) appealed to Abu Bakr to compile all the verses of the Quran into one book to protect it from being lost.

The companions understood the importance of preserving the Quran. Abu Bakr created a committee of the twelve companions who were most knowledgeable about the Quran. The committee was led by the talented scribe of Prophet Muhammad ﷺ, Zayd ibn Thabit (*radi Allahu anhu*). Senior companions such as Ali ibn Abi Talib, Uthman ibn Affan, and Umar ibn al-Khattab (*radi Allahu anhum*) were also members of the committee. They collected all of the pieces of leather and other materials that had verses of the Quran written on them. They recited, double-checked, and recorded all of the Quran's 6,236 verses, in the order that Angel Jibril had specified to Prophet Muhammad ﷺ before he passed away.

When the committee finished putting all the verses together in the correct order, they were copied onto gazelle skin by Sa'id ibn al-As (*radi Allahu anhu*), who was known for his beautiful handwriting, and recited out loud in an open meeting with many *huffaz* present. There was no objection from anyone—they all agreed the Quran had been written down correctly. A total of 33,000 companions agreed that the written Quran matched what they memorized.

This copy was saved with the caliph. Later, seven copies were made from the original book and sent to different parts of the Islamic empire, like Damascus and Yemen. Some of these copies still exist and are on display at Topkapi Palace in Istanbul and other museums. There is not a single difference between the Quran recited around the world today and these original copies, because the Quran has been preserved in the hearts of Muslims.

Years later, when more people embraced Islam, non-Arabs struggled to read the Quran because the Arabic letters did not have any dots or vowel marks on them. Another committee was created to add the dots and vowel marks, which made it easier for people who didn't speak Arabic to read the Quran.

Muslims recite the Quran all around the world, and if someone makes even the slightest mistake, it is noticed, because Muslims know the

Quran very well. The Quran is recited from beginning to end in mosques all around the world each Ramadan, and all recitations match the first copy put together 1,400 years ago.

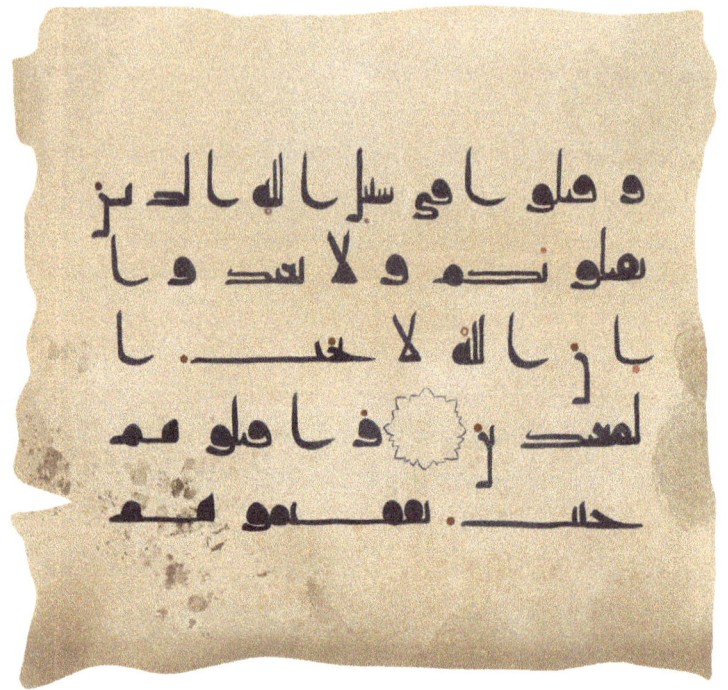

> ### Practical Application Questions
> - Think of a time when you were responsible for your chores and homework. After you did what you said you would, how did that build others' trust in you? How did you feel?
> - List ways our actions and decisions can create consequences.
> - Describe the characteristics you can see in a responsible person.

7. Maintaining Ties of Kinship

How Do We Maintain Ties of Kinship?

Maintaining ties of kinship means staying connected with our family members, like our grandparents, aunts, uncles, and cousins. It means loving, helping, and checking on our relatives, even if they live far away. It doesn't matter if our family members are different from us; we can stay connected with them no matter what their religion or manners. Allah ﷻ has commanded us to maintain our ties of kinship and promised us a great reward in this life and the hereafter when we do.

How Did the Prophet ﷺ Maintain Ties of Kinship?

- Prophet Muhammad ﷺ respected his relatives, even when they hurt him and said cruel things to him in public. He did not hold any grudges against them and always forgave them for their hurtful actions.
- He ﷺ advised them and helped them follow the right path toward Janna.
- He ﷺ made *dua* for them and was there for them when they needed help.
- He ﷺ was grateful for everything they did for him and did everything he could to show them his appreciation.

Maintaining Ties of Kinship in Action

A Difficult Family Meal

Three years after the message of Islam was first revealed to the Prophet ﷺ, Allah ﷻ commanded him to begin inviting his close relatives to the religion. Prophet Muhammad ﷺ and his wife Khadija (*radi Allahu anha*) invited all their relatives to a meal and cooked delicious food for them. When they finished eating, Prophet Muhammad ﷺ began to tell them about Islam. Suddenly, his uncle Abu Lahab rudely interrupted him and ordered him to stop.

The Prophet ﷺ had worked hard with Khadija to prepare for this gathering so he could teach them about Islam, but he respected his uncle regardless of his rudeness. He remained silent and did not argue with him.

Prophet Muhammad ﷺ did not let his uncle's disrespectful behavior hold him back from following Allah's commands, though. A few days later, he invited his relatives to another meal. Even though Abu Lahab had prevented him from teaching about Islam at the first meal, the Prophet ﷺ invited him again. Prophet Muhammad ﷺ respected and cared for him because he was his uncle.

This time Prophet Muhammad ﷺ asked them: "Have I ever told you a lie?"

They said, "We have never heard you tell a lie."

He then started explaining the message of Islam. He told them to worship only Allah ﷻ and warned them about continuing to worship idols. He told his family that he had been sent by Allah ﷻ to guide them and all humankind to Janna.

Safiyya (*radi Allahu anha*), the Prophet's aunt, was happy to hear this news. She believed him right away and embraced Islam. She had known there was something special about the Prophet ﷺ ever since he was a little boy.

His uncle Abu Lahab, on the other hand, was very angry to hear this. He tried to convince people that if other tribes heard about this new religion, they would fight them. "I will never support you in this!" Abu Lahab yelled at the Prophet ﷺ.

Abu Talib, who was another uncle of the Prophet's ﷺ, and a great leader of Mecca, stopped his brother Abu Lahab and said, "I will always support Muhammad ﷺ." Abu Talib had promised his father, Abdul Muttalib, that he would take good care of little Muhammad ﷺ, no matter what—and he did just that until the last day of his life.

Eventually Prophet Muhammad ﷺ began spreading the message of Islam to all of Mecca. Many people did not like this and wanted him to stop. They wanted people to continue worshipping their false gods and idols. The leaders of Mecca were furious and did everything they could to stop the new religion from spreading. They were afraid that Mecca would lose its power and status among the Arab tribes. Prophet Muhammad's people were very mean to him, but he ﷺ was always patient with them and cared for them, regardless of their behavior. He maintained the ties of kinship with his family and the people of Mecca by teaching them, advising them, being patient with them, and making *dua* that they be guided to the right path. And alhamdulillah, most of them eventually were.

Why do you think Prophet Muhammad ﷺ invited Abu Lahab to another family meal, even though he was very rude the first time?

A Clever Plan

Prophet Muhammad ﷺ encouraged his companions to maintain ties of kinship with their family members, regardless of their religion. He honored those who respected and cared for their relatives.

When Prophet Muhammad ﷺ announced the message of Islam, some of his family members became Muslim. Some, however, refused to believe in him and even tried to stop him from teaching people about Allah ﷻ. There were also some relatives who did not accept Islam themselves but still defended the Prophet ﷺ from any harm, like his beloved uncle Abu Talib, who protected the Prophet ﷺ until the last day of his life.

When the people of Quraysh made an agreement to **boycott** the Muslims, some Meccan leaders did not approve, such as Hisham ibn Amr and Mut'im ibn Adi. They supported the Prophet ﷺ even though they never embraced Islam. They respected the ties of kinship between themselves and the Prophet ﷺ. They always defended the Prophet ﷺ and helped out when the Muslims were being **oppressed** in Mecca.

Hisham ibn Amr could not bear the idea of harming those who were related to him. He did not listen to the leaders of Mecca and did his best to provide the Muslims with food during the boycott. He didn't care if he got in trouble with the Meccans—he wanted his relatives to be saved from hunger.

One day, he thought of a brilliant plan. In the morning, he took his **mules** to the Valley of Abu Talib—where the Muslims were forced to stay during the boycott—so they could memorize the road. Then he sent the mules back to the valley when it was dark, carrying food on their backs for the Muslims. He was able to do this several times before he was caught by the Quraysh. When they learned that he had broken the rules, they captured him. Once he was freed, he sent his mules back to the valley with more food for the Muslims. He did this night after night until he was caught by the Quraysh again.

The leaders of Quraysh asked him, "Why are you doing this? You're just getting yourself in trouble."

Hisham replied, "How can I abandon my relatives? How can I eat while they are starving?"

After the great victory at the Battle of Badr, Prophet Muhammad ﷺ consulted his companions on what to do with the prisoners they had captured. Some companions thought they should ransom them, while others thought they should be killed. At that moment, Prophet Muhammad ﷺ remembered Mut'im ibn Adi, who had passed away some time before, and told his companions that if Mut'im had asked him to set all the captives free, he would have done so. The Muslims finally agreed to set a ransom for each captive, but the Prophet's ﷺ respect for Mut'im ibn Adi, who honored family ties, shows us how important that honor is.

How did Hisham ibn Amr use mules to help him? How do you think he was caught?

Your Family Matters

In the early days of announcing the message of Islam, Prophet Muhammad ﷺ was faced with **rejection** from his own uncle, Abu Lahab, who used many **tactics** to prevent the Prophet ﷺ from preaching about Islam. Abu Lahab had two sons, Utba, who was married to the Prophet's daughter Ruqayya, and Utayba, who was married to his ﷺ daughter Umm Kulthum (*radi Allahu anhum*). Abu Lahab commanded his sons to divorce the Prophet's daughters and send them back home. He had hoped this distraction would stop the Prophet ﷺ from inviting people to Islam.

When Mecca was liberated years later, Prophet Muhammad ﷺ entered the city as the leader. Everyone wondered what he would do with the people who had hurt the Muslims in the past. Some came to the Prophet ﷺ and embraced Islam, while some were too ashamed to face him. To their surprise, the Prophet ﷺ declared his forgiveness to all the people of Mecca.

Soon after, the Prophet ﷺ was talking with his uncle al-Abbas (*radi Allahu anhu*): "Oh Abbas, where are the two sons of your brother [Abu Lahab]? Why do I not see them?" Al-Abbas informed him that they had left with some of the other Meccans.

The Prophet ﷺ said: "Go and and bring them to me."

When they arrived, the Prophet ﷺ invited them to Islam. They embraced it and he forgave them for what they had done in the past. He held their hands, took them to the Kaaba, and made *dua* for them. When he came back, his face was lit up with joy.

Despite what Abu Lahab and his sons did to the Prophet ﷺ and his daughters, they were still his family, and Prophet Muhammad ﷺ cared about their religion and fate. He modeled for us how to maintain ties of kinship by demonstrating forgiveness and **compassion**, even toward relatives who had hurt him.

Practical Application Questions

- Think of a time when a distant family member called you on Eid. How did you feel? How does it feel to be connected to your family members? How might it be different if you talked to them more often?
- List ways to stay connected to family members who live far away.
- Describe the characteristics you can see in a person who maintains ties of kinship.

8. Courage

What Is Courage?

Courage is facing your fears by doing the right thing even when it's difficult. Having courage is not the same thing as being fearless. It's about facing your fears head-on. Having courage also means trying new things. When you are courageous, you challenge yourself to achieve your goals, and you trust that Allah ﷻ will help you and guide you.

How Did the Prophet ﷺ Practice Courage?

- Prophet Muhammad ﷺ stood up for what was right, even when there was a risk he would get hurt.
- He ﷺ did not let the fear of failure stop him; he kept trying until he succeeded.
- He ﷺ always acted bravely to protect others.
- Prophet Muhammad ﷺ had the courage to spread the message of Islam regardless of what the Quraysh said.
- When living in Mecca was no longer safe for the Muslims, Prophet Muhammad ﷺ took the courageous step of migrating to a new land so they could practice their religion freely.

Courage in Action

A Tale of Bravery

When Umar ibn al-Khattab (*radi Allahu anhu*) embraced Islam, Prophet Muhammad's mission took a new course in history. Umar was a leader in Mecca and had a unique character that brought pride and strength to Islam. He embraced Islam at a time when it was still being practiced secretly because the people of Quraysh were trying to stop Muslims from worshipping one God.

When Umar embraced Islam, he went to Dar al-Arqam, where Prophet Muhammad ﷺ and his companions used to meet, to recite his *shahada* with the Prophet ﷺ. He was the fortieth person to become a Muslim. Prophet Muhammad ﷺ was overjoyed because he had asked Allah ﷻ for Umar to embrace Islam one day. Allah ﷻ had accepted his *dua* and made it true. Everyone at Dar al-Arqam celebrated his *shahada* by shouting "Allahu akbar!"—forgetting that they needed to keep quiet so no one would hear them! They were extra-excited because another Meccan leader, the beloved uncle of Prophet Muhammad ﷺ, Hamza ibn Abdul Muttalib (*radi Allahu anhu*), had also embraced Islam just three days before.

As soon as Umar became Muslim, he asked the Prophet ﷺ, "Oh Messenger of Allah ﷺ, aren't we upon the truth?"

Prophet Muhammad ﷺ said, "Yes, we are!"

Umar said, "Then why are we hiding from the people of Mecca? Let's go out and declare our faith!"

Prophet Muhammad ﷺ agreed and lined up the Muslims in two lines: one behind Umar and one behind Hamza. This would be the first time that the Muslims went out and declared their faith in public. Because the Muslims were behind two strong Meccan leaders who had embraced Islam, no one dared hurt them.

That was not enough for Umar, though. He wanted everyone in Mecca to know he had become a Muslim. He wasn't afraid of the Quraysh or of what anyone might do. He went to a man who was known for spreading rumors and told him that he had accepted Islam. The man shared the news near the Kaaba, where everyone in Mecca gathered. The people of Mecca were so angry when they heard this news that they tried to attack Umar. He was strong and courageous; no one was able to take him down. Then a man from Mecca told them to leave him alone.

That night, Umar thought to himself, *"Who would be the most bothered by me becoming a Muslim?"* He realized it must be Abu Jahl, his uncle. He did not want to wait until morning, so he went to his house and knocked on the door.

Abu Jahl opened the door and said, "Welcome, my dear nephew!"

Umar said, "I wanted to let you know that I believe in Allah ﷻ and His Messenger, Prophet Muhammad ﷺ."

Abu Jahl was so angry that he slammed the door in Umar's face.

This is the courage that Umar ibn al-Khattab showed from his first day as a Muslim until the last day of his life. He brought victory and pride to the Muslims because of his bravery. Umar's courage helped the Muslims announce their faith without fear of being hurt by the people of Mecca. The Muslims had previously been prevented from praying around the Kaaba, but Umar made them feel safe enough to start praying there. Despite the **opposition** they faced, the Muslims remained strong in their faith.

Courage at the Kaaba

Abdullah ibn Mas'ud (*radi Allahu anhu*) was one of the first believers who embraced Islam. He was very close to Prophet Muhammad ﷺ. Abdullah (*radi Allahu anhu*) knew the Quran very well. His recitation was among the most beautiful. Even though he was not as strong as the other companions, he had a lot of courage.

Prophet Muhammad ﷺ wanted the people of Mecca to hear the Quran. He gathered his companions to discuss the idea of reciting the Quran near the Kaaba for the first time. Who would recite? Many *sahaba* (companions of the Prophet ﷺ) were suggested. The Muslims wanted to choose someone who either had a strong tribe to protect them or was strong enough to defend themselves.

Abdullah ibn Mas'ud was the last person anyone would think of. He was not from a powerful tribe, and he did not have a large or strong body to defend himself. But he was courageous. Abdullah ibn Mas'ud **insisted** that he be the one to recite the Quran at the Kaaba, even after the other companions tried to talk him out of it.

Abdullah went to the Kaaba in the middle of the day and started reciting the beautiful **ayas** of **Surat al-Rahman** with his amazing voice. When the people of Mecca heard him reciting the Quran, they attacked him and hurt him. They didn't stop until the companions came and rescued him.

*It is the Lord of Mercy who taught the
Quran. He created man and taught him
to communicate. Quran 55:1–4*

The companions asked him, "Why did you do that, Abdullah? We told you they would hurt you!"

Abdullah said, "I wanted to be the first to recite the Quran at the Kaaba. And I will do it again tomorrow!"

Prophet Muhammad ﷺ was proud of Abdullah and told him that would be unnecessary—he had already completed their mission by reciting Quran to the Meccans.

Defender of the Prophet ﷺ

Nusayba bint Ka'ab (*radi Allahu anha*) was one of the first people of Yathrib to embrace Islam. She had taken up archery at a very young age and was very good at it. She was known for her courage and the great character she demonstrated many times throughout Islam.

During the Battle of Uhud, the Meccan army was attacking the Muslim army, and Prophet Muhammad's life was in danger. Nusayba rushed in with her sword and shield and fought valiantly to protect the him. Later, Prophet Muhammad ﷺ mentioned that whatever direction he turned on the battlefield, he found Nusayba defending and protecting him. Prophet Muhammad ﷺ was amazed by her outstanding courage.

Practical Application Questions

- Think of a time when you had the courage to try something new, even when it was difficult. What happened? How did it make you feel?
- List ways your self-esteem can affect your courage.
- Describe the characteristics you can see in a courageous person.

9. Fairness

What Is Fairness?

Fairness means treating others the way you would like to be treated. Being fair means following the rules and never cheating. This gives everyone a chance to succeed. We act fairly when we take turns and share with others; this helps everyone feel welcome and included. A fair person treats everyone with kindness and respect, even if they are quite different from them.

How Did the Prophet ﷺ Practice Fairness?

- Prophet Muhammad ﷺ was always fair and reasonable.
- He ﷺ was open-minded and listened to other people's opinions.
- He ﷺ made decisions based on evidence rather than emotions.
- If two people came to the Prophet ﷺ for judgment, he would listen to both sides before forming an opinion.
- He ﷺ always gave people a chance.
- He ﷺ followed the rules, even in his own family.
- He ﷺ never took advantage of others or blamed them.

Fairness in Action

The Beloved One

Zayd ibn Haritha (*radi Allahu anhu*) was from one of the tribes of Yemen. When he was a young boy, he was kidnapped while on a trip with his mother and taken to the slave market in Mecca. He wound up serving the Prophet ﷺ, who loved him like his own son. He referred to him as his Beloved. Zayd grew up in the Prophet's household learning about fair treatment and good **morals** from him.

Meanwhile, Zayd's father, Haritha, was looking for Zayd everywhere. He would go from tribe to tribe, spreading the news, sharing his description, and asking about him. At Hajj time one year, a man recognized Zayd in Mecca. When he returned to his tribe, this man informed Zayd's father that he was living as a servant to a man named Muhammad.

Haritha and his brother traveled to Mecca to meet the Prophet ﷺ. When they arrived, they heard about the Prophet's manners and hoped that he would return Haritha's son to him. Haritha approached Prophet Muhammad ﷺ and said, "Oh Muhammad, you come from a noble family. You are known for your fairness. Our son was taken away from us and sold into slavery. Zayd is our son! We ask you to give him back to us, and we will give you money in return."

After Prophet Muhammad ﷺ listened carefully to the father, he said: "I need to ask Zayd first and let him decide. If he chooses to go back to you, you can take him without paying anything. If he chooses to stay with me, then he is welcome to stay. I will not force him to go with you."

Prophet Muhammad ﷺ loved Zayd dearly but was willing to see him go back to his family if that's what would make him happy. Haritha was thrilled with this solution and agreed. The Prophet ﷺ brought Zayd and asked if he knew the two men. He said, "Yes, this is my father and uncle." The Prophet ﷺ explained the situation and offered the choice to Zayd. When Zayd chose to stay with the Prophet ﷺ, his father was shocked.

"I cannot believe you would choose slavery over living with your own family!" he shouted.

Zayd said, "How can I choose anyone over the Prophet ﷺ? I have never met anyone like him before."

Prophet Muhammad ﷺ was happy when he heard Zayd's words. He stood up and announced: "Oh people of Mecca, I declare Zayd free, and I adopt him as my own son."

The Prophet's words calmed Zayd's father, as he saw that his son was loved and cared for and was now freed from slavery. Zayd was called Zayd ibn Muhammad for years, until a verse was revealed by Allah ﷻ in the Quran about adoption. Allah ﷻ commanded that adopted children should keep the names of their biological fathers, so that they would know their true origins.

ٱدْعُوهُمْ لِآبَآئِهِمْ هُوَ أَقْسَطُ عِندَ ٱللَّهِ

*Let your adopted children keep their family names.
That is more just in the sight of Allah. Quran 33:5*

Despite the Prophet's love for Zayd, he didn't let his emotions control his actions.

Fair Share

Prophet Muhammad ﷺ demonstrated fairness in his life with everyone around him. When he established rules, he always applied them to himself first.

When the Muslims were going to the Battle of Badr against the *mushrikun* (disbelievers), they had only seventy camels to ride, but over three hundred men. The Prophet ﷺ suggested that every three men share one camel. They would take turns: One would ride and the other two would walk, then they would switch.

Prophet Muhammad ﷺ was assigned a camel with his cousin, Ali ibn Abi Talib, and his companion, Abu Lubaba (*radi Allahu anhuma*). Ali and Abu Lubaba offered to walk for the entire trip so Prophet Muhammad ﷺ could ride the camel. They respected the Prophet ﷺ and could not imagine him walking while they rode. He was the Messenger of Allah ﷺ! He was also much older than them—they were in their early twenties, while he was in his fifties. They worried about him getting tired.

When it was time to travel, Ali and Abu Lubaba told the Prophet ﷺ that he should ride the camel the entire time. They said, "Oh Messenger of Allah, we will walk, and you will ride."

Prophet Muhammad ﷺ smiled and replied gently, saying: "The two of you are not any younger or stronger than I am, and I am not in any less in need of the *ajr* [reward] than the two of you."

Even though he was the leader, the Prophet ﷺ was always **humble** and fair. He explained to them that he was doing this for the sake of Allah's ﷻ pleasure, just like they were. This is just one way Prophet Muhammad ﷺ demonstrated fairness, justice, and equality, and these qualities were one reason he was loved and respected by everyone around him.

The Stolen Shield

When the Muslims settled in Medina, Prophet Muhammad ﷺ began establishing the new city. He wrote the **constitution** of Medina, which made several agreements between the Muslims and the other tribes who were already living in Medina, including several Jewish tribes. One of the laws said "All Muslims shall unite against the one who does injustice—even if it is one of them." The Constitution of Medina also had laws that gave each tribe the right to practice their religion freely.

The Constitution of Medina demonstrates the fairness of Prophet Muhammad ﷺ as a leader. Prophet Muhammad ﷺ respected the Jews as an important part of their community. He respected their rights as well, giving them full independence in dealing with their own matters.

The Jews of Medina had their own laws and, even though they had the right to solve their own problems, they preferred asking for Prophet Muhammad's judgment when they had an argument among themselves. The Jews were so impressed by his sense of justice and fairness that they asked him to solve their **disputes** for them according to their Jewish laws.

One day, a Jewish man was **accused** of stealing a shield that belonged to a Muslim. The shield had been kept inside a sack that had some powder in it. A trail of powder led all the way to the house of the accused Jewish man, but he said he was innocent. He said that he did not steal the shield.

Prophet Muhammad ﷺ listened carefully to both sides before deciding the case. Even though all the evidence seemed to point to the man being guilty of stealing the shield, Prophet Muhammad ﷺ spoke to all of the witnesses and **investigated** further to make sure his decision was fair.

In the end, they found a man who **confessed** to stealing the shield and putting it in the Jewish man's house. The Jewish man was innocent. He was impressed by the Prophet's fairness and thankful for his determination to apply justice. The Prophet ﷺ was fair to everyone, regardless of who they were or what religion they followed.

What could have happened if Prophet Muhammad ﷺ didn't investigate the case of the stolen shield?

Practical Application Questions

- Think of a time when someone was unfair to you. What happened? How did it make you feel?
- List ways that you can be fair to others.
- Describe the characteristics you can see in a fair person.

10. Generosity

What Is Generosity?

Generosity means being willing to give to and share with others. Generosity can be sharing snacks with your classmates or donating toys and clothes to those in need. Generosity can also be setting aside time to listen to your friend who needs to talk or giving someone a hug to cheer them up. A generous person is happy to give food, time, kind words, and money—all while being humble and grateful to Allah ﷻ.

How Did the Prophet ﷺ Practice Generosity?

- Prophet Muhammad ﷺ modeled the best ways to be generous to others.
- He ﷺ was generous with his neighbors, always sharing food with them and taking care of them when they were sick.
- He ﷺ was regularly engaged in serving others.
- He taught us the ethics of donating to others by giving them the best items, providing a sense of **dignity** to those in need.
- He always praised generosity and promised great rewards from Allah ﷻ to motivate us.
- Prophet Muhammad ﷺ expressed his gratitude for Allah's blessings through giving and showing compassion to others.

Why do you think Prophet Muhammad ﷺ taught us to donate the *best* items, rather than old or gross things? *Hint: How would you feel if you were in need and someone gave you something ripped or dirty?*

Generosity in Action

The Freed Slave

Abu Bakr al-Siddiq (*radi Allahu anhu*) was the first man outside of the Prophet's family to embrace Islam. He had been the Prophet's best friend ever since they were little boys. Abu Bakr was known for his kind heart. He always helped the poor and needy. He was a smart businessman in Mecca. When he embraced Islam, he didn't miss any opportunity to spend his money in support of the Prophet ﷺ and the Muslims. One time, he even donated all his money to support the Muslims.

In the early days of Islam, the leaders of Mecca hurt anyone who embraced Islam, especially those who did not belong to a strong tribe, and this included slaves. Slaves had to obey their masters and do whatever they were told to do. They had no one to protect them from the **harsh** leaders of Mecca. Abu Bakr used his money to buy Muslim slaves from their cruel masters and freed them for the sake of Allah ﷻ.

Umayya ibn Khalaf was a leader of the Quraysh. He owned a slave named Bilal ibn Rabah (*radi Allahu anhu*). Bilal became a Muslim, and once his master found out, he started hitting him. His master wanted him to go back to worshipping the idols. No matter how hard Umayya hit Bilal, he would never leave Islam.

His master would say, "Just leave Islam and I'll stop hurting you!"

But Bilal would always reply, "*Ahadun, ahad.*" (There is only one God, only one God.)

One day, Abu Bakr passed by Umayya ibn Khalaf and saw him making Bilal lie on the hot desert sand. He was placing a big rock on Bilal's chest, trying again to get him to leave Islam. Abu Bakr was sad and angry for Bilal and decided to help him. He offered Umayya a huge amount of money to buy Bilal, and Umayya was happy to sell him. *Let me get rid of Bilal. He doesn't obey my commands anyway*, Umayya thought to himself. Abu Bakr paid Umayya and set Bilal free. Abu Bakr's generosity saved Bilal's life.

Bilal played such an important role in Islam! Have you heard of him? If you have, can you remember what he is known for? *We will read more about Bilal in Chapters 14, 18, and 19.*

The Gift of Giving

Prophet Muhammad ﷺ always wore his finest clothes for Jumu'a (Friday prayers). He always took a bath and put on his best perfume before the prayer. After noticing that Prophet Muhammad's Friday cloak had holes in it, one of the companions gave the Prophet ﷺ a beautiful, new robe.

The next Friday Prophet Muhammad ﷺ wore the new robe, and on his way to the masjid, two of his companions came to greet him. One of them said, "Oh Messenger of Allah ﷺ, how beautiful is your garment! Can you please give it to me as a gift?"

Prophet Muhammad ﷺ, who was known for his generosity and for never letting anyone down, gave him the new robe without a second thought. Then Prophet Muhammad ﷺ went back home to put on his old cloak.

While he was gone, the companions said to the man, "Why did you ask the Prophet ﷺ for his new garment? Don't you know that he only has two robes? He likes to wear the nice one to Jumu'a."

The man went to the Prophet ﷺ and asked him to take his new robe back, but Prophet Muhammad ﷺ insisted that he should keep it. The companion was very happy to keep this special cloak, gifted to him by Prophet Muhammad ﷺ. He took care of it and kept it until the last day of his life.

This is how our beloved Prophet ﷺ demonstrated generosity with everyone around him.

Uthman's Well

Uthman ibn Affan (*radi Allahu anhu*) was one of the first believers to embrace Islam. He was a wealthy businessman and always spent his wealth to support Prophet Muhammad ﷺ and the message of Islam. Even after he migrated to Medina, he continued to help the Muslims in every way he could. Whenever Prophet Muhammad ﷺ asked for donations, he would be one of the first to offer his wealth for the sake of Allah ﷻ.

The only source of fresh drinking water in Medina was a well that was owned by a Jewish man who charged a lot of money for the water. This made life very difficult for the Muslims. Prophet Muhammad ﷺ cared about the Muslims and wanted to solve this problem.

He asked his companions: "Who will buy this well for the Muslims in exchange for a well in Janna?"

With no **hesitation**, Uthman ibn Affan said he would buy the well and allow the Muslims to drink from it for free. Uthman went to the Jewish man and offered to buy the well, but he refused to sell it. Uthman didn't want to give up, so he offered to buy half of the well. The man agreed, knowing that Uthman was a great businessman and that he would benefit from being his partner. Uthman and the Jewish man decided to take turns "owning the well." Uthman would own it one day, and the Jewish man would own it the next.

When it was Uthman's turn, Muslims would get their water for free, so no one would buy water when it was the Jewish man's day to own the well. The man could not understand why Uthman always gave the water for free on his days, even though he had paid a lot of money for the well. Little did he know that Uthman was providing the water to the Muslims in return for a well in Janna, which is far more valuable than what the Jewish man was earning.

The Jewish man offered to sell the other half of the well to Uthman, and he agreed. The man asked for 20,000 dirhams, and although that was a lot of money, Uthman agreed to pay the full amount.

Several years later, Uthman was offered an extremely large amount of money for the well, but he would not sell it. He said, "Allah ﷻ will reward me ten times what I give in charity." Uthman never sold the well to anyone. He wanted to earn the best reward from Allah ﷻ by providing free water so the Muslims could drink.

The well, which is called Rooma, has been preserved until today and is known as Bi'r Uthman. Over the years, many palm trees have grown around it. All the dates that are harvested from these trees are donated under the name of Uthman ibn Affan. Recently, the Saudi Arabian government took charge of Uthman's well and charity. They created a bank account under his name and split the yearly income into one part for charity and one part for investments. The money was used to purchase land around **al-Masjid al-Nabawi**, and a hotel was built on it. Most of the income from this hotel is donated in charity to **orphans** and **widows**. The trust for Uthman's charity has generated millions of dollars over the years. Uthman's generosity and his reward have lasted more than 1,400 years!

Practical Application Questions

- Think of a time when someone wouldn't share with you. How did that make you feel? What would you tell your future self if you didn't feel like sharing?
- List ways generosity can help our community.
- Describe the characteristics you can see in a generous person.

11. Confidence

What Is Confidence?

As believers, we can have confidence in two ways: in ourselves and in Allah ﷻ. Self-confidence means believing in our own abilities and feeling positive about who we are. We can grow our confidence by being kind to ourselves. Confidence in Allah ﷻ means trusting His plan, even when it's hard for us in the moment, and trusting that He ﷻ always wants what's best for us. We have certainty, or **yaqeen**, in Allah's love for us, and this gives us strength during hard times.

How Did the Prophet ﷺ Practice Self-Confidence and Confidence in Allah ﷻ?

- Prophet Muhammad ﷺ was confident about himself and always had a positive attitude.
- He ﷺ always trusted in Allah's plan for him and his *ummah*.
- He ﷺ was proud of Islam and was able to set goals to spread the message successfully.
- When people had a negative opinion of him ﷺ, he did not let it stop him from spreading his message.
- Prophet Muhammad ﷺ taught us how to deal with our mistakes. He would admit his mistakes and learn from them.
- He ﷺ stood up for his beliefs—no matter how hard it was.

Confidence in Action

In the Face of Opposition

For years, Muslims were **persecuted** by the people of Mecca, who bullied and harmed them because they worshipped one God. The Quraysh always plotted against the Muslims and tried to hurt them. Eventually, Mecca was no longer a safe place for the Muslims and the Prophet ﷺ knew that he needed to find a new place to spread the message of Islam.

During **Dhul Hijja** each year, Arab tribes would come from different parts of the Arabian Peninsula to perform the Hajj. Prophet Muhammad ﷺ would visit these tribes in their tents, inviting them to the religion of Islam. He would ask the leaders to welcome Muslims onto their land, help defend them against harm, and spread the message of Islam to all of their people. He approached these leaders with great confidence in himself, as he was the Messenger of Allah ﷻ. Even though most of the tribal leaders didn't treat him well, he remained confident in his message and beliefs.

The Quraysh did not want people to help the Muslims. They wanted to keep the Muslims in Mecca, where they could continue oppressing them. Abu Lahab, the Prophet's uncle, would follow Prophet Muhammad ﷺ every time he went to speak to the leaders of different tribes, throwing rocks at him and saying, "Don't listen to him, he's a liar!"

People believed Abu Lahab because he was the Prophet's uncle. They thought, "If his uncle is saying he's a liar, then why would we accept him in our land? His tribe doesn't even believe him."

Abu Jahl, one of the Quraysh's leaders, would also walk around and warn people about the Prophet ﷺ, saying, "Don't listen to this man, he is just trying to make you stop worshipping the idols."

Nothing they did or said affected the Prophet's confidence in himself. He was certain in Allah ﷻ and stood up for what he believed in. He had hope and confidence in Allah's plan for himself, his family, and his companions. He trusted that Allah ﷻ would help the Muslims find safety. Prophet Muhammad ﷺ continued to talk to the tribes until he met a group from Yathrib (which would later be called Medina) who happily welcomed the Muslims to their land and promised to defend the message of Islam.

A King's Open Arms

There was a time when it was increasingly dangerous for Muslims to live in Mecca. The leaders of Mecca decided they would do anything to stop the Prophet ﷺ from spreading the message of Islam. They were very cruel to the Muslims, hurting them so much that eventually they couldn't stand it any longer. They asked the Prophet ﷺ for help. He told them to migrate to a safer place that would allow them to practice their faith without fear. He told them to go to Abyssinia, which was ruled by a just and fair king called al-Najashi. This king would not oppress anyone living on his land.

A group of eleven men and four women traveled to Abyssinia and were welcomed by the Abyssinian people. The rest of the Muslims stayed in Mecca and continued to practice their faith despite the challenges. Sometime later, Quraysh sent Amr ibn al-As and Abdullah ibn Abi Rabia (*radi Allahu anhuma*) to bring the Muslims back to Mecca. They brought expensive gifts to bribe the king and his ministers. They told al-Najashi that the Muslims were troublemakers and asked him to expel the Muslims from Abyssinia and send them back to Mecca. But before making a decision, al-Najashi asked to hear the other side of the story.

Prophet Muhammad's cousin Ja'far ibn Abi Talib (*radi Allahu anhu*), who represented the Muslims, stood in front of the king with great confidence in his religion. His confidence helped him move the king's heart during his speech.

"Oh King, we were living in Mecca and worshipping idols and fake gods. We were mean to our families and neighbors. We were unfair to each other. Then Allah ﷻ sent us a prophet, Prophet Muhammad ﷺ. We knew him to be honest and trustworthy. He taught us to do good. He taught us that idols cannot help us and that we need to worship Allah ﷻ alone. He taught us to be kind to our relatives and neighbors. We followed Prophet Muhammad ﷺ, but our relatives did not like it and tried to force us to worship idols again. They were cruel and hurt us. So we came to you, knowing that you are a just king and are fair to everyone around you."

The king was impressed by Ja'far's words. He asked him to recite some verses of the Quran. Ja'far chose to recite beautiful verses from **Surat Maryam** that speak about Isa (*alayhi al-salam*). Al-Najashi was moved to tears and said, "It appears that these words and the words that were revealed to Jesus are from the same source." Al-Najashi recognized that the words of the Quran were indeed the words of God.

قَالَ إِنِّى عَبْدُ ٱللَّهِ ءَاتَىٰنِىَ ٱلْكِتَٰبَ وَجَعَلَنِى نَبِيًّا ۝ وَجَعَلَنِى مُبَارَكًا أَيْنَ مَا كُنتُ وَأَوْصَٰنِى بِٱلصَّلَوٰةِ وَٱلزَّكَوٰةِ مَا دُمْتُ حَيًّا ۝

Jesus declared, "I am truly a servant of Allah. He has destined me to be given the Scripture and to be a prophet. He has made me a blessing wherever I go, and bid me to establish prayer and give zakat as long as I live. Quran 19:30–31

As a last attempt, Amr ibn al-As went to the king the following day and said: "Oh King, ask the Muslims what they say about Isa, son of Maryam." He accused the Muslims of disrespect toward Isa. So al-Najashi called for them. The Muslims were worried about how the king would react when they answered his question about Isa, but they decided to say the truth that Allah and His Messenger had brought.

When they arrived, the king asked them: "What do you say of Isa, son of Maryam?"

Ja'far ibn Abi Talib said: "We say that which has come to us from our Prophet, that he [Isa] is the servant of Allah, His prophet, His spirit, and His word who was created by the command of Allah."

Upon hearing that, the king asked Amr ibn al-As to take his gifts back and said he would not expel the Muslims from his land. Instead, he granted them security and peace. The Muslims were safe, and the king was very kind to them.

In Allah's Care

When the time for **hijra** (migration from Mecca to Medina) came, Prophet Muhammad ﷺ and his best friend, Abu Bakr (*radi Allahu anhu*), had to secretly leave Mecca at night. The people of Mecca did not notice that he had left until the morning. They became furious and did everything they could to bring the Prophet ﷺ and his friend back to Mecca. The Meccans offered a reward of one hundred camels to anyone who brought them back—dead or alive. People looked for them everywhere, hoping to win the reward.

Prophet Muhammad ﷺ and Abu Bakr were heading to Medina, taking a different path than the normal route, which led straight to Medina. They hid in a cave called **Thawr** and stayed there for three days. Eventually, a group of Meccans reached the area of the cave, and Prophet Muhammad ﷺ and Abu Bakr could hear them getting closer and closer. They got so close that Abu Bakr said to the Prophet ﷺ, "If these men look down, they will see us." Abu Bakr feared that they would take the Prophet ﷺ and kill him. Tears fell from his eyes.

Prophet Muhammad ﷺ told him calmly, "Do not be sad. Indeed, Allah ﷻ is with us." Prophet Muhammad ﷺ had confidence in Allah ﷻ and trusted that He would protect them from danger.

Little did they know that Allah ﷻ had sent a spider to cover the entrance of the cave with its web. He ﷻ also sent a pigeon to build a nest and lay eggs in front of the cave. This convinced the Meccans that the cave was empty, so they didn't look inside.

"Don't waste your time here. Let's leave and look somewhere else," one of the men said.

Prophet Muhammad ﷺ and Abu Bakr were relieved to see them leave. No matter how hard the situation became, they were confident in Allah ﷻ and knew He ﷻ would always take care of them.

Practical Application Questions

- Think of a time when you achieved a goal you had been working on. What happened? How did it make you feel about yourself?
- List ways that social media can affect your confidence.
- Describe the characteristics you can see in a confident person.

12. Grit

What Is Grit?

Grit is the ability to continue working toward a goal even when faced with failure or difficulties. No matter how hard things get, you keep trying your best. Having grit means you are willing to keep working to reach your goal even when things get tough. Doing your best and relying on Allah ﷻ will help you develop grit and overcome all of your challenges.

How Did Prophet Muhammad ﷺ Demonstrate Grit?

- Prophet Muhammad ﷺ had grit when dealing with challenges and failure.
- He ﷺ always had a positive attitude and did not waste time feeling sorry for himself. He knew that Allah ﷻ would reward him for his actions, no matter the outcome.
- Prophet Muhammad ﷺ never gave up on spreading the message of Islam. He used each setback as a lesson.
- Prophet Muhammad ﷺ was able to see the funny side when facing difficulties, like when Suhayb al-Rumi (*radi Allahu anhu*) had an eye infection and was eating dates. The Prophet ﷺ joked with him to make him feel better and said: "How can you eat dates with an infected eye?"
- Whenever Prophet Muhammad ﷺ was faced with failure, he would quickly bounce back and take action instead of making excuses or blaming others.
- Prophet Muhammad ﷺ stayed focused and used **coping mechanisms** to deal with challenges.

 What are coping mechanisms? List some coping mechanisms that you have used before.

Grit in Action

Unshakable Courage

When Prophet Muhammad ﷺ declared the message of Islam, the people of Mecca were very mean and cruel to the Muslims. They could not pray around the Kaaba because Quraysh would hurt them. Prophet Muhammad ﷺ didn't let their cruel actions stop him, though, and he continued to pray at the Kaaba. When he would walk to the Kaaba, the people of Quraysh would throw stones at him and put thorns in his path for him to step on.

Prophet Muhammad ﷺ was praying near the Kaaba one day when the leaders of Quraysh saw him. They were furious because nothing they had done stopped him from praying. Abu Jahl, a cruel leader of Mecca, suggested throwing the guts of a dead camel on the Prophet's back while he was making **sujud** (bowing down in **prostration**). They agreed and threw the rotten guts on the Prophet ﷺ during his prostration. The Prophet ﷺ was not able to move because of how heavy the guts were.

The Meccans laughed and made fun of him. He stayed in that position, unable to move, until his daughter Fatima (*radi Allahu anha*), saw him. She removed the **filth** from his back and yelled at the people for doing that to her father. Even though she was just a little girl at the time, her grit allowed her to defend her father. When Prophet Muhammad ﷺ saw the tears in his beloved daughter's eyes, it hurt him so much. He comforted her and told her not to worry; Allah ﷻ would spread the message of Islam no matter what they did.

Prophet Muhammad ﷺ was able to see the bright side in this situation instead of feeling sorry for himself or complaining. He had determination that kept him moving forward, regardless of all the difficulties he faced.

12. GRIT

How did Fatima demonstrate grit when she defended her father ﷺ?

The Boycott

When the people of Quraysh had done everything they could think of to stop Prophet Muhammad ﷺ from spreading the message of Islam, they made a plan to stop the Muslims once and for all. The leaders of Mecca decided to boycott Prophet Muhammad ﷺ, his clan Banu Hashim, and his followers. "No one should buy from the Muslims or sell them any food. That way, they will either starve or go back to worshipping idols," said one of the Meccan leaders. They also agreed not to marry any Muslims or have any business dealings with them unless they either left Islam or handed over the Prophet ﷺ. They wrote the agreement on a piece of paper with the phrase **"bismika Allahumma"** (with Your name, oh Allah) on top. Each leader signed it, and they hung it inside the Kaaba to keep it safe.

The leaders of Mecca thought the boycott would make the Muslims leave Islam and give up, but the Muslims did not let anything stop them. They were forced to stay in the Valley of Abu Talib, which was on the outskirts of Mecca, away from their houses and belongings. When they went to the city to buy food, the people of Mecca would not sell them anything to eat. As the days went by, the situation became very difficult for the Muslims. They did not have enough food, so they shared the little bit they had with one another. The Muslims become weaker and weaker. Sometimes they had to eat leaves to survive.

For three years, the Muslims were patient and never gave up. They had the grit to maintain their faith and not hand over the Prophet ﷺ to the leaders of Mecca. They had faith that Allah ﷻ would reward them for their patience and for enduring such hardship. Their goal was to protect the Prophet ﷺ and to worship Allah so they could enter Janna. Their faith and trust in Allah ﷻ motivated them to keep going.

Prophet Muhammad ﷺ always made *dua*, asking Allah ﷻ to help the Muslims. One day, Allah ﷻ sent Angel Jibril (*alayhi al-salam*) to tell the Prophet ﷺ that the paper on which the Quraysh had agreed to the boycott had been eaten by bugs—everything except for the phrase "*bismika Allahumma.*"

Abu Talib believed what Prophet Muhammad ﷺ had learned from Angel Jibril and told the leaders of Quraysh. Abu Talib said, "If my nephew is right, you must cancel the boycott. If he is wrong, I will hand him over to you."

The leaders of Mecca were excited that Muhammad ﷺ had finally given up, especially since some of the Meccans were publicly asking to stop the boycott. The leaders were sure nothing had happened to the paper—it was safe inside the Kaaba after all.

When they opened the Kaaba door, they were shocked to see that what the Prophet ﷺ had said was true. The paper had been eaten by bugs, except for the very top with the phrase *"bismika Allahumma"* written on it. The leaders of Quraysh were forced to cancel the boycott and allow the Muslims to go return to their homes.

Even though the people of Mecca witnessed this miracle, they *still* refused to believe that Prophet Muhammad ﷺ was the Messenger of Allah ﷻ. They said he was just a magician.

The Worst Day

When Aisha (*radi Allahu anha*) asked Prophet Muhammad ﷺ about the worst day of his life, he told her it was the day he went to Ta'if and was rejected by the people there.

He visited Ta'if during the Year of Sorrow, the year in which his uncle Abu Talib and his wife Khadija (*radi Allahu anha*) had passed away. They were his biggest supporters. Abu Talib supported him in the community, and Khadija supported him at home. She comforted him during the difficult times in Mecca.

Even though the Prophet ﷺ had lost some of his closest supporters and the Muslims had become weak after the difficult years of the boycott, Prophet Muhammad ﷺ never gave up on his goal of spreading Islam. He did, however, begin looking for a new place for the Muslims to live. The first place he thought of was Ta'if, the city closest to Mecca.

Prophet Muhammad ﷺ secretly left Mecca for Ta'if with his beloved adopted son, Zayd ibn Haritha (*radi Allahu anhu*). They traveled by foot to avoid any trouble from the people of Mecca, who might have become suspicious if they saw that the Prophet's camel was missing. When they arrived, Prophet Muhammad ﷺ met with the three leaders of Ta'if, who were brothers. He told them about Allah ﷻ and Islam. He asked them to convert to Islam and to welcome the Muslims to their city. He had hoped that they would protect the Muslims from the Quraysh. Instead, one of the leaders called him a liar, while a second mocked, "Couldn't Allah ﷻ find anyone better than *you* to be his prophet?"

The Prophet ﷺ agreed to leave Ta'if and asked only that they not tell the Quraysh that he had been there. His grit kept him determined to spread the message of Islam and find a safe place for the Muslims. He was not willing to give up, despite all of the obstacles he was facing.

As the Prophet ﷺ was leaving Ta'if, the leaders sent a group of people to kick him out of the city, mocking him and throwing stones. Even children threw rocks at Prophet Muhammad ﷺ and Zayd, who loved the Prophet ﷺ dearly and tried his best to protect him. The Prophet's feet were hurt from the stones and were bleeding badly. Zayd was bleeding too. They finally reached a garden wall and sat under a tree to rest. Prophet Muhammad ﷺ was deeply saddened by what had happened, but he did not let failure or difficulties stop him. He knew Allah ﷻ would always help him reach his goal. He made a beautiful *dua*, asking Allah ﷻ to help him:

> Oh Allah, I complain to You of my lack of strength, and my helplessness and lowliness before men. You are the Most Merciful and the Lord of those who are humble and weak, and You are my Lord. To whom do You leave me? To a stranger who will treat me harshly [Ta'if]? Or to a close relative to whom You have given power over me [Abu Lahab]?
>
> As long as You are not angry with me, I do not worry. Your protection is better for me. Oh Allah, I seek refuge in Your Face, which is the source of the light that gets rid of the darkness and because of which this world is guided. And I seek refuge in Your Face that Your anger should come down upon me. It's Your right to criticize until You are content. And there is no power nor strength except with You and through You.

The Prophet Muhammad ﷺ and Zayd went back to Mecca more determined than ever. Prophet Muhammad ﷺ did not waste his time complaining and feeling sorry for himself. He pushed forward and came up with a new plan to spread the message of Islam. He trusted Allah ﷻ.

Practical Application Questions

- Think of a time when you developed grit by setting a goal and pushing forward, even though it was difficult. How did it feel when you reached your goal in the end?
- List ways you can build grit.
- Describe the characteristics you can see in a person with grit.

13. Honesty

What Is Honesty?

Honesty means being truthful in what you say and do. An honest person tells the truth even when it's tough or scary. They tell the truth without hiding any details or making anything up. An honest person also acts truthfully, without tricking others. When we are honest, we build trust with our friends and family because they know they can count on us.

How Did the Prophet ﷺ Practice Honesty?

- Prophet Muhammad ﷺ always spoke the truth. Even the people of Quraysh said they never heard him tell a lie.
- People called him ﷺ the Honest and the Trustworthy even before he became a prophet.
- Prophet Muhammad ﷺ admitted when he was wrong.
- When he ﷺ spoke, he did not **exaggerate** the facts.
- His ﷺ words were truthful, even when he was joking.

Honesty in Action

The Best Deal

Suhayb al-Rumi (*radi Allahu anhu*) was an Arab who grew up in Rome. He came to Mecca without any money, but he was slowly able to become one of the greatest businessmen there. He was one of the early believers in Islam and practiced Islam secretly with Prophet Muhammad ﷺ.

At the time of the hijra, Prophet Muhammad ﷺ allowed the Muslims to leave Mecca and migrate to Yathrib. Suhayb tried to migrate with the Muslims, but the people of Quraysh locked him up and would not let him leave. So he was stuck there, unable to join Prophet Muhammad ﷺ and the rest of the companions.

One day, he was able to run away, and he headed toward Medina. The Quraysh noticed he was gone and caught up with him. They called out to him and yelled, "You came to us with nothing! You got rich in Mecca! Do you think we are going to let you leave with all your wealth?" Suhayb had actually hidden all his wealth somewhere around Mecca.

Suhayb replied, "If I tell you where all my money is, will you let me go to Medina?"

The people of Quraysh agreed to the deal. They knew that Prophet Muhammad's ﷺ companions did not lie. They let him go after he told them exactly where he had hidden his wealth. And they found it exactly where he said it would be.

Suhayb made his way to Medina to join the Prophet ﷺ and his companions. When the Prophet ﷺ saw him approaching from afar, he said: "*Rabiha bay Aba Yahya!*" (Indeed, you have profited [by giving everything away]!)

Suhayb gave away all his wealth because joining the Prophet ﷺ was more valuable to him than money. A verse in the Quran was revealed praising him and promising him Janna. Suhayb truly made the best deal.

And there are those who would dedicate their lives to Allah's pleasure. And Allah is Ever Gracious to [His] servants. Quran 1:207

This story is called "The Best Deal." What is a deal? What deal did Suhayb make?

"Will I Go to Janna?"

Prophet Muhammad ﷺ would not tell a lie, even when he was telling a joke. He would joke with his family all the time to bring joy and laughter to the house. His jokes were beautiful and truthful. He told jokes to make others feel better and to create a bond with those around him. He did not allow people to tell jokes that would embarrass others.

An old woman once came to the Prophet ﷺ and asked him, "Oh Messenger of Allah, will you ask Allah ﷻ to let me enter Janna?"

Prophet Muhammad ﷺ replied that *old* women do not enter Janna. The woman started to become angry and asked him ﷺ what he meant.

The Prophet ﷺ explained that only *young* women will enter Janna, because Allah ﷻ will make everyone young again. She laughed and left with a wide smile.

Prophet Muhammad ﷺ was the best example of honesty, even in his humor.

The Bracelets of Kisra

When things became too difficult for the Prophet ﷺ and the Muslims in Mecca, Allah ﷻ allowed them to migrate to Medina. Prophet Muhammad ﷺ left secretly at night with his best friend, Abu Bakr (*radi Allahu anhu*). In the morning, when the people of Mecca realized that the Prophet ﷺ had left, they announced a large prize of one hundred camels for anyone who brought him ﷺ back, dead or alive.

Suraqa ibn Malik (*radi Allahu anhu*) could recognize the signs people left as they walked or rode camels through the desert sand. He began following the tracks of the Prophet ﷺ and Abu Bakr, and gained on them quickly. But just as they came into sight, Suraqa's horse suddenly sank into the sand and flipped him over. Smoke appeared in front of him, and he could no longer see the Prophet ﷺ.

He pulled out his *azlam*, a set of divining arrows used by idol worshippers. The arrows had answers written on them, like "Proceed" and "Do not proceed," and he thought the idols would communicate to him what he should do based on which arrow he drew from the quiver. He pulled out an arrow; it said "Do not proceed." He ignored it because he wanted to win the one hundred camels. He got back on his horse, but the same thing happened again, and they both fell into the sand. After falling down for a third time, he knew that he should not try to capture the Prophet ﷺ.

He asked permission from the Prophet ﷺ to come closer and talk to him. He told them he would not hurt them. When he reached the Prophet ﷺ, Suraqa offered to help them. The Prophet ﷺ asked him to cover their tracks and said: "Oh Suraqa, how will you be the day you put on the bracelets of Kisra [Khosrow]?"

Suraqa was shocked. "Kisra, the emperor of Persia? I am going to wear his bracelets?" Kisra was known for the beautiful gold he wore.

Suraqa could not believe what the Prophet ﷺ had said to him. That one day he would wear the bracelets of the mightiest man on Earth!

Several years later, Suraqa embraced Islam and moved to Medina. After the Prophet ﷺ passed away, Abu Bakr (*radi Allahu anhu*) became the first caliph. When Umar (*radi Allahu anhu*) became the caliph next, he liberated the Persian Empire. A box was brought to Umar and it was filled with the bracelets of Kisra. Umar called for Suraqa ibn Malik (*radi Allahu anhu*). Everyone knew about the Prophet's promise to him. Umar asked Suraqa to sit in his chair, and he put two bracelets on his wrist. Everyone shouted: "Allahu akbar! The Prophet's promise is now true!"

The companions kept the Prophet's promise and delivered the bracelets of Kisra to Suraqa.

Practical Application Questions

- Think of a time when you chose not to be honest. What happened? How did it make you feel? What would you say to yourself the next time you feel afraid to be honest?
- List ways being honest (or not being honest!) can affect the community.
- Describe the characteristics you can see in an honest person.

14. Inclusivity

What Is Inclusivity?

Inclusivity means including everyone and not leaving any person or group behind. Inclusive people do not **exclude** those who are different from them. Inclusivity happens when we understand that every one of us is a creation of Allah ﷻ. When we try to see other people's points of view, we can appreciate our differences and uniqueness.

How Did the Prophet ﷺ Practice Inclusivity?

- Prophet Muhammad ﷺ was accepting of those who were different from him.
- He ﷺ never made negative comments about others or judged their backgrounds or ethnicities.
- He ﷺ was open to meeting new people who were different from him, and he ﷺ tried to find things in common.
- Prophet Muhammad ﷺ always consulted his companions and respected different opinions.
- He ﷺ put a stop to negative comments about others' ethnicities, gender, race, or differences.

Inclusivity in Action

The Pledge of al-Aqaba

For years, Muslims in Mecca remained patient while they endured difficulties and harm. The leaders of Mecca committed every evil action they could think of to stop the Muslims from worshipping one God. No matter what they did, though, the Muslims never gave up and continued to worship Allah ﷻ alone. They knew that Allah ﷻ would never abandon them.

Prophet Muhammad ﷺ understood that Mecca wasn't safe for Muslims, so he searched for other tribes to welcome the Muslims into their land. Each year he would talk to the leaders of the tribes that came to Mecca for Hajj, telling them about the message of Islam. He was hoping one would welcome and protect the Muslims.

Allah ﷻ had prepared a special land for the Muslims. This land was called Yathrib (later Medina), a beautiful place filled with palm trees. In Yathrib, there were many tribes; some were Arab, and some were Jewish. The Jews were expecting a final prophet to come soon because it was mentioned in their book, the Torah. They expected him to be Jewish, but little did they know that the final prophet would actually be an Arab.

Eleven years after the first revelation of the Quran, six Arab men from Yathrib went to Hajj. While they were in Mecca, they heard about a man who claimed to be a prophet. When they met him, he explained that he was Allah's final prophet and that Allah ﷻ had sent him with the Holy Quran. They were amazed by his character and believed in him right away! They promised that they would teach the people of Yathrib about Islam and invite them to the religion. They also promised to meet with the Prophet ﷺ again the following Hajj.

14. INCLUSIVITY

The next year, the number of Muslims in Yathrib had grown to twelve. When they came for the Hajj, they met with the Prophet ﷺ at a place called al-Aqaba. There, they agreed to worship Allah ﷻ alone, do good deeds, and not commit any evil or harm. They promised to follow Prophet Muhammad ﷺ and protect him. This was called the First Pledge of al-Aqaba. After completing the pledge, the Muslims from Yathrib promised the Prophet ﷺ that they would return once again to see him during the following Hajj.

One year later, the Muslims from Yathrib returned to Mecca again to meet with the Prophet ﷺ, but now their number had grown to seventy-five, including two women! Prophet Muhammad ﷺ welcomed the two women, Asma and Nusayba (*radi Allahu anhuma*), and included them in the important meeting where the history of both Yathrib and Islam took a great turn.

It was not common in pre-Islamic times for women to be involved in important meetings, but Prophet Muhammad ﷺ valued and included everyone. The new Muslims agreed to welcome the Prophet ﷺ and the Muslims of Mecca to their land. They agreed to worship Allah ﷻ alone, do no evil, follow the Prophet ﷺ, and protect him. This became known as the Second Pledge of al-Aqaba.

Prophet Muhammad ﷺ demonstrated the importance of inclusivity in Islam by respecting and honoring the opinions of both men and women on every occasion.

A Blessed Sip

When Prophet Muhammad ﷺ first arrived in Medina, he paired each **Muhajir** (a Muslim who had migrated from Mecca) with an Ansar (a Muslim originally from Medina). This way, every Muslim from Mecca would be given a place to stay where they would be taken care of and have someone to help them.

As the years passed, more and more people embraced Islam and migrated to Medina. The number of Muhajirun kept growing until all the houses in Medina reached their capacity. There wasn't enough room for any more people to live in the houses.

Prophet Muhammad ﷺ came up with a solution—a **shelter** would be built behind his mosque, al-Masjid al-Nabawi. This shelter was called **al-Suffa**. Everyone who migrated to Medina was welcome to stay in the shelter. Eventually, forty people lived in al-Suffa. Prophet Muhammad ﷺ took care of the people there and dedicated a lot of time to helping them. He always encouraged the *sahaba* to support the people of al-Suffa in every possible way. Prophet Muhammad ﷺ respected and valued them. He included them in each **event** and loved to share his food with them.

Prophet Muhammad ﷺ noticed that Abu Hurayra (*radi Allahu anhu*), one of the people of al-Suffa, looked weak from not eating. Abu Hurayra did not have any money to buy food, so Prophet Muhammad ﷺ invited him to come to his house. Prophet Muhammad ﷺ asked his wife Aisha (*radi Allahu anha*) if they had any food in the house. She said, "All we have is a glass of milk that our neighbor sent us." Abu Hurayra was happy that there was finally something for him to drink, but Prophet Muhammad ﷺ asked him to call all the people of al-Suffa to come and join them. He wanted to include them all in the sharing of the milk.

Abu Hurayra did what he was told, but he wondered how one glass of milk would be enough for forty people. The people of al-Suffa all gathered at the door of the Prophet's house and entered one by one, drinking from the glass of milk until they were completely satisfied. When it was Abu Hurayra's turn to come in, he was surprised to see the glass of milk was even more full than before. Prophet Muhammad ﷺ offered the glass to him and asked him to drink. Every time he stopped drinking, Prophet Muhammad ﷺ would ask him to drink more and more, until Abu Hurayra was full.

Prophet Muhammad ﷺ himself drank from the cup of milk after he had made sure that everyone from al-Suffa was full. This story shows how much Prophet Muhammad ﷺ cared about the people of al-Suffa—he even shared his only glass of milk with them—and through a miracle of Allah ﷻ, it was enough for everyone.

The First Muezzin

When we think of the **adhan** (call to prayer), we remember Bilal ibn Rabah (*radi Allahu anhu*), the first **muezzin** ever. The muezzin is the person who calls Muslims to prayer by reciting the *adhan* before the five daily prayers at the mosque.

Bilal ibn Rabah was one of the most trusted and loyal companions of the Prophet ﷺ. He was one of the first believers to embrace Islam, even though it was dangerous for him to do so as a slave.

Bilal was from Ethiopia. He was born into slavery and lived in Mecca, where slaves had no rights or protection. They had to do what their masters told them, no matter what.

Bilal was freed by Abu Bakr (*radi Allahu anhu*), who bought him from his master while he was being tortured and set him free. Bilal then joined the Prophet ﷺ and the community of Muslims as a free man. He was always by the Prophet's side. Whenever the Prophet ﷺ needed to be left alone, he would ask everyone to leave except for Bilal. The Prophet ﷺ loved Bilal and gave him a special **rank**, even though they lived in a society where slaves had the lowest status in the community.

Prophet Muhammad ﷺ included Bilal in all discussions and events. Prophet Muhammad ﷺ did not care about his skin color or his background. He loved Bilal for his intelligence, faith, and sincerity. Umar ibn al-Khattab (*radi Allahu anhu*) would call him, "our master, who was freed by our master," referring to Abu Bakr.

When the new mosque in Medina was built, Abdullah ibn Zayd (*radi Allahu anhu*) told the Prophet ﷺ he had a dream in which a man in green garments taught him the words to the *adhan*. Prophet Muhammad ﷺ knew this was a vision from Allah ﷻ and said Bilal ibn Rabah would be the muezzin—the one who would call for prayer.

Whenever the Prophet ﷺ went to the mosque for his daily prayers, Bilal would recite the *adhan*, calling people to come for prayer. He would wake the Prophet ﷺ before Fajr and ask his permission before calling the *adhan*.

Bilal was the perfect person for this honor because even when his cruel master tried to make him leave Islam, Bilal refused and said the only words he knew about Allah ﷻ—"One, one!" The *adhan* that testifies to the oneness of God with "**La ilaha illallah**" was to be called by Bilal, who endured such hardship but kept his faith in Allah ﷻ.

Years later, Prophet Muhammad ﷺ and the Muslims liberated Mecca (*Fath Makka*). The Prophet ﷺ entered Mecca with ten thousand Muslims and visited the Kaaba for the first time since the believers had been forced to leave Mecca and migrate to Medina. He entered as the leader of Mecca. Once the Prophet ﷺ reached the Kaaba, he called for Bilal. He asked him to climb the Kaaba and call the *adhan* for the very first time in Mecca. Bilal stood on top of the Kaaba and declared the oneness of Allah with his strong voice in the same city where he used to be a slave, while everyone in Mecca watched. The people of Mecca were **astonished** to see a slave climb the Kaaba and be the one to call every single person to prayer.

Prophet Muhammad ﷺ was showing the Meccans the society he had created. Our beloved Prophet ﷺ stood against racism 1,400 years ago. He showed everyone that a person's status is not based on their skin color or lineage, but based on their faith.

The companions learned from the Prophet ﷺ to respect Bilal regardless of his background or skin color. After the Prophet ﷺ passed away, Umar ibn al-Khattab went to al-Aqsa Mosque in Jerusalem to receive its keys. Umar asked Bilal to call the *adhan* for the first time there as well.

So Bilal was not only the first muezzin; he was also the first to call the *adhan* at three different sacred mosques.

Practical Application Questions

- Think of a time when you practiced inclusivity at school or saw someone else be inclusive. What happened? How did it make others feel?
- List different ways you can be inclusive.
- Describe the characteristics you can see in an inclusive person.

15. Loving for the Sake of Allah

What Is Loving for the Sake of Allah ﷻ?

Loving for the sake of Allah ﷻ means caring about someone for no other reason than pleasing Allah ﷻ. This kind of love is sincere because we are not expecting to gain anything in return other than Allah's pleasure. When we love others for the sake of Allah ﷻ, we can become closer to one another and closer to Him ﷻ.

How Did the Prophet ﷺ Demonstrate Loving for the Sake of Allah ﷻ?

- Prophet Muhammad ﷺ encouraged us to declare our love for Allah's sake to one another.
- Prophet Muhammad ﷺ promised us that when Muslims love each other for Allah's sake, their friendship will last longer—they will even be together on the Day of Judgment.
- Those who love each other sincerely for Allah's sake will be invited under the shade of His **throne** on the Day of Judgment.
- Prophet Muhammad ﷺ encouraged his companions to love for Allah's sake on many occasions.

Loving for the Sake of Allah ﷻ in Action

A New Kind of Brotherhood and Sisterhood

After Prophet Muhammad ﷺ arrived in Medina, he focused on building the new Muslim community. This was the first time Muslims had had the freedom to practice Islam in public. Prophet Muhammad ﷺ was a great leader and he took care of every aspect of the community in

Medina. First, a masjid was built so the Muslims could gather and pray. Next, Prophet Muhammad ﷺ focused on the Muhajirun, the Muslims who had migrated from Mecca. They had nowhere to stay and had left everything behind: their wealth, their houses, and their businesses.

Prophet Muhammad ﷺ came up with a brilliant idea: He created a social bond between the Muhajirun and the Ansar (the Muslims who already lived in Medina). He paired each Muslim from the Muhajirun with a Muslim from the Ansar as brothers and sisters in Islam. This social system of sisterhood and brotherhood became the foundation of the Muslim community in Medina. It solved problems for both the Muhajirun and the Ansar. The Ansar shared their wealth and homes with the Muhajirun, who had left behind everything in Mecca, and the Muhajirun shared their knowledge of Islam with the Ansar, who were new Muslims and needed to learn their religion.

A special kind of relationship soon developed between Muslims in Medina—the Ansar and the Muhajirun's selfless and generous actions translated into love for the sake of Allah ﷻ.

The sincere love that grew between the companions for Allah's sake allowed them to lead the *ummah* with **righteousness** and justice after the passing of Prophet Muhammad ﷺ.

Prophet Muhammad ﷺ Misses You

Prophet Muhammad ﷺ loved his companions dearly, but one time when he was with a group of them he expressed how much he missed someone else: "I wish I could meet my brothers and sisters," he said.

The companions wondered what the Prophet ﷺ meant. "Are we not your brothers?" they asked.

Prophet Muhammad ﷺ said: "You are my companions, but my brothers are those who will have faith in me even though they have not seen me."

The Messenger of Allah ﷺ cared for and loved all of his followers—even those who believed in him after he passed away and did not have the chance to meet him. He was sitting with his companions 1,400 years ago, thinking about his *ummah*—those who followed him without even seeing him. He wished to be with *you*! Yes, *you* believe in him and follow his **sunna**, even though you have never met him.

The Sword of Allah ﷻ

Khalid ibn al-Walid (*radi Allahu anhu*) was one of the greatest **commanders** in Islam. Prophet Muhammad ﷺ gave him the title Sayfullah (the Sword of Allah ﷻ) for his bravery and courage in battle. He is known for his brilliant battlefield tactics and his many victories.

Khalid ibn al-Walid was the son of al-Walid ibn al-Mughira, a Meccan leader who was opposed to Islam. Before Khalid embraced Islam, he followed his father's lead, fighting against Prophet Muhammad ﷺ and the Muslims. He even led the disbelievers against the Muslims in the Battle of Uhud, where the Muslims were defeated, Prophet Muhammad ﷺ was injured, and many Muslims were killed.

Later, after learning about Prophet Muhammad's message, Khalid ibn al-Walid felt the desire in his heart to embrace Islam. He went to the Prophet ﷺ with his friend, Amr ibn al-As (*radi Allahu anhu*), and the Prophet ﷺ accepted them with open arms. He welcomed them lovingly, without questioning their previous actions toward the Muslims. That is true love for the sake of Allah ﷻ, and the Prophet's ﷺ companions were able to witness it.

All the companions congratulated Khalid and Amr and welcomed them. The companions embodied loving for Allah's sake by not holding grudges against Khalid and Amr.

From that day forward, Khalid dedicated his life to defending the Muslims. He helped protect the message of Islam until his last day. Stories about his courage and bravery have lasted through the generations—proving his sincere love for Islam, the Messenger ﷺ, and Allah ﷻ.

Prophet Muhammad ﷺ and his companions embodied loving for the sake of Allah ﷻ when they welcomed Khalid and Amr with open arms. What other character traits do you think the Prophet ﷺ and his companions embodied when they did this?

Practical Application Questions

- Think of a time when you met a new person and loved them for the sake of Allah ﷻ. How did you feel? How can loving someone for the sake of Allah ﷻ make a relationship stronger?
- List ways to show our love of the Prophet ﷺ.
- Describe the characteristics you can see in a person who loves you for the sake of Allah ﷻ.

16. Honoring Our Parents

How Can We Honor Our Parents?

Honoring our parents means being grateful to them for all they have done for us. It means understanding that nothing we do can ever pay them back for all the difficult years they spent raising us. We honor our parents when we treat them with respect and kindness. This means being patient with them and not upsetting them by saying rude words or hurting their feelings. Allah ﷻ mentioned the importance of honoring and pleasing our parents in the Quran.

وَوَصَّيْنَا ٱلْإِنسَٰنَ بِوَٰلِدَيْهِ حَمَلَتْهُ أُمُّهُۥ وَهْنًا عَلَىٰ وَهْنٍ وَفِصَٰلُهُۥ فِى عَامَيْنِ أَنِ ٱشْكُرْ لِى وَلِوَٰلِدَيْكَ إِلَىَّ ٱلْمَصِيرُ

We have commanded people to be good to their parents: their mothers carried them, with strain upon strain, and it takes two years to wean them. Give thanks to Me and to your parents—all will return to Me. Quran 31:14

وَٱعْبُدُوا۟ ٱللَّهَ وَلَا تُشْرِكُوا۟ بِهِۦ شَيْـًٔا وَبِٱلْوَٰلِدَيْنِ إِحْسَٰنًا وَبِذِى ٱلْقُرْبَىٰ وَٱلْيَتَٰمَىٰ وَٱلْمَسَٰكِينِ وَٱلْجَارِ ذِى ٱلْقُرْبَىٰ وَٱلْجَارِ ٱلْجُنُبِ وَٱلصَّاحِبِ بِٱلْجَنۢبِ وَٱبْنِ ٱلسَّبِيلِ وَمَا مَلَكَتْ أَيْمَٰنُكُمْ إِنَّ ٱللَّهَ لَا يُحِبُّ مَن كَانَ مُخْتَالًا فَخُورًا

Worship God; join nothing with Him. Be good to your parents, to relatives, to orphans, to the needy, to neighbors near and far, to travelers in need, and to your servants. God does not like arrogant, boastful people. Quran 4:36

In these verses, Allah ﷻ tells us that pleasing our parents is a way of worshipping Him.

How Did the Prophet ﷺ Demonstrate How to Honor One's Parents?

- Prophet Muhammad ﷺ encouraged us to honor our parents and promised us happiness in this life and the hereafter when we do. Prophet Muhammad ﷺ was an orphan, but he honored everyone who cared for him when he was young.
- He ﷺ encouraged the companions to please their parents—even those whose parents stood against Islam. No matter what their parents did, the companions always remained respectful to them.
- When the companions asked Prophet Muhammad ﷺ about the most beloved deeds to Allah ﷻ, he said praying on time and honoring your parents.

Honoring Our Parents in Action

Honoring the Past

Prophet Muhammad ﷺ was an orphan; his father, Abdullah, passed away before he was born, and his mother, Amina, passed away when he was six years old. He was then cared for by his grandfather, Abdul Muttalib. His grandfather also passed away, and finally he was moved to the care of his uncle, Abu Talib.

Abu Talib had many children, but he did not have much money. He loved the Prophet ﷺ dearly and took good care of him; he would not let his children eat dinner until Prophet Muhammad ﷺ had joined them. Abu Talib noticed how special little Muhammad ﷺ was, and he felt blessed to have him in his house. Abu Talib's wife, Fatima bint Asad (*radi Allahu anha*), cared dearly for the Prophet ﷺ as well. Even though she was his **foster parent**, she treated him like he was her own son.

Prophet Muhammad ﷺ was grateful to Abu Talib and Fatima for raising him and taking good care of him. When he married Khadija (*radi Allahu anha*), he showed his gratitude to them by offering to foster their son, Ali ibn Abi Talib (*radi Allahu anhu*). Ali lived with the Prophet ﷺ for many years, and Prophet Muhammad ﷺ helped raise him.

16. HONORING OUR PARENTS

Whenever Prophet Muhammad ﷺ visited Fatima bint Asad, he treated her with kindness and respect. He also named his beloved daughter Fatima in honor of her. When Fatima passed away, Prophet Muhammad ﷺ cried and remembered how she used to share her food with him when he was hungry and how she took care of him when he was sick. He ﷺ made *dua* for her, covered her with his robe, and asked Allah ﷻ to reward her for all that she had done for him.

How did Prophet Muhammad ﷺ honor Abu Talib and Fatima bint Asad?

A Righteous Son

A woman came to the Prophet ﷺ with a young boy. She said, "This is my son, Anas. I would like him to live with you and serve you." The Prophet ﷺ agreed, and Anas ibn Malik (*radi Allahu anhu*) began living with him. Anas was able to learn about every aspect of Islam while also earning Allah's reward for serving the Prophet ﷺ.

One day, Anas's mother came to the Prophet ﷺ complaining about him, saying, "My son refuses to eat with me from the same plate!"

Prophet Muhammad ﷺ asked Anas about this. Anas said that the reason he had stopped eating from the same plate as his mother was that he feared eating a piece of food she wanted to eat. He did not want to be disrespectful to his mother, even accidentally! Prophet Muhammad ﷺ praised Anas for being a righteous son, and his mother was also proud of him, as he was clearly learning wonderful things from the Prophet ﷺ, including the importance of respecting his parents and making sure not to hurt their feelings.

Choosing Family

Uways al-Qarani (*radi Allahu anhu*) embraced Islam while living in Yemen. He loved Prophet Muhammad ﷺ and wanted to have the honor of meeting him and joining the ranks of the *sahaba*, but he was very busy taking care of his mother. His mother needed a lot of help because she was blind and weak. And she had no one to take care of her except Uways.

Knowing the importance of honoring parents in Islam—and the great reward that comes with it—Uways chose to stay with his mom and take care of her when delegations from Yemen went to Medina to see the Prophet ﷺ. He chose to give up the status of being a *sahabi* (companion).

His love for the Prophet ﷺ was so sincere that Angel Jibril (*alayhi al-salam*) told Prophet Muhammad ﷺ about him, and the Prophet ﷺ could feel his love from far away. Prophet Muhammad ﷺ **predicted** that he would never meet Uways in person. But he knew that after he passed away, Uways would come to perform Hajj and meet Umar ibn al-Khattab (*radi Allahu anhu*).

He told Umar that Uways would come one day to Medina from Yemen, and that Umar should ask Uways to make *dua* for him. He ﷺ described Uways and told Umar about his mother and how sick she was. The Prophet ﷺ said that the way he treated his mother made him a righteous person, and the *dua*s of righteous people are answered.

Whenever there was a caravan of travelers from Yemen, Umar ibn al-Khattab would ask them if a man named Uways was with them. Years after the Prophet ﷺ had passed away, Umar finally met him. He had taken care of his mother until she passed away, and he was finally able to travel to Medina. Umar explained to Uways what Prophet Muhammad ﷺ had predicted about him and asked him to make *dua* for him.

Honoring our parents can help us achieve righteousness, just like Uways.

16. HONORING OUR PARENTS

Practical Application Questions

- Think of a time when you were patient with your parents when they asked you to help with household chores. How did you show your respect for them? How did that make them feel?
- List ways we can honor our parents.
- Describe the characteristics you can see in a person who honors their parents.

17. Teamwork

What Is Teamwork?
Teamwork means working with others respectfully to reach a goal. Working in a team requires respect, self-control, and cooperation. Teamwork means being there for your team members, trying your best, and working together to achieve your objectives. Allah ﷻ blesses us when we collaborate with others to do good deeds, and He will lead us to success.

How Did the Prophet ﷺ Practice Teamwork?
- Prophet Muhammad ﷺ modeled amazing teamwork in many aspects of his life.
- Prophet Muhammad ﷺ was a kind leader who considered his team members' opinions. He taught us to be united and promised us a great reward for working together as a group.
- Prophet Muhammad ﷺ encouraged us to support one another in order to become a strong and united *ummah*.
- He ﷺ never asked people to do things that he did not do himself. He would be the first to get to work and complete a task with the team.

Teamwork in Action

Building a New Masjid in Medina
When Prophet Muhammad ﷺ arrived in Medina, he bought land to build a new mosque for the Muslims to pray in and gather in. This was the second mosque built in Medina and was later called al-Masjid al-Nabawi.

Even though Prophet Muhammad ﷺ was fifty-three years old at the time, he helped build the masjid with his companions. Clay was mixed with water and left in the sun to harden into large bricks. Prophet Muhammad ﷺ carried the heavy bricks with the companions while reciting a *dua* asking for the Muhajirun and the Ansar to be blessed by Allah ﷻ. He chanted the *dua* to make the work easier. The companions chanted with him as they all worked together.

اللَّهُمَّ لَا عَيْشَ إِلَّا عَيْشُ الآخِرَةِ فَاغْفِرْ لِلْأَنْصَارِ وَالْمُهَاجِرَهْ

*Allahumma la aysha illa aysh al-akhira
faghfir lil-ansar wal-muhajira.*

Oh Allah, there is no true life except
the life of the hereafter, so have mercy
on the Ansar and the Muhajirun.

Prophet Muhammad ﷺ demonstrated the spirit of cooperation and teamwork among the companions by being a helpful leader.

Muslims from Mecca and Medina were able to come together and build al-Masjid al-Nabawi, which stands in Medina to this day. The tomb of Prophet Muhammad ﷺ is located in the masjid, under the green dome that was built during the Ottoman era in 1837 CE. Though al-Masjid al-Nabawi has had many **expansions** over the years, the original structure exists because of Prophet Muhammad's leadership and the companions' teamwork—1,400 years ago.

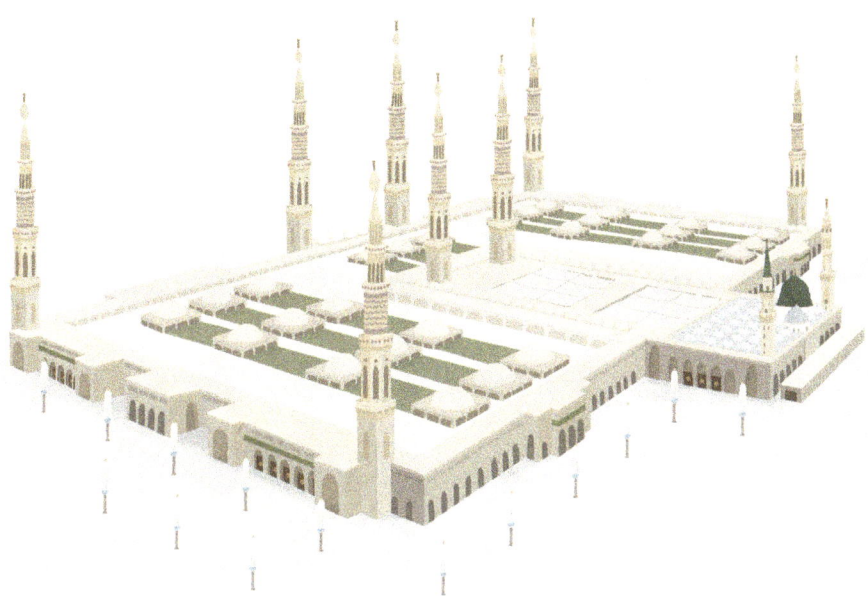

Al-Masjid al-Nabawi began as a small and humble mosque 1,400 years ago. Today, it is the second largest mosque in the world and can hold one million people!

Seeds of Freedom

Salman al-Farisi (*radi Allahu anhu*) was from Persia. The people there worshipped fire, but he didn't believe this was the right religion. After traveling to many places searching for the True God, he heard about a new prophet in Medina. A monk told him there were three signs by which he would be able to recognize this new prophet.

1. The new prophet would *not* eat food given as charity.

2. He *would* eat food given as a gift.

3. He would have the **seal of prophethood** between his shoulders.

Salman joined a caravan that was heading to Medina, hoping to meet the new prophet, but he was captured along the way and sold as a slave.

While he was collecting dates from a palm tree one day, he overheard his master talking about a man who had come from Mecca claiming to be a prophet. Salman could not believe his ears. He immediately came down from the tree and asked, "What are you saying? Who is that man coming from Mecca?"

His master hit him and said, "That is none of your business! Get back to work!"

That night, Salman secretly went to meet the Prophet ﷺ and check for the signs of prophethood. He collected whatever dates he had and gave them as charity to the Prophet ﷺ. The Prophet ﷺ accepted the dates, but he would not eat them. That was the first sign!

The next day, Salman gave him some dates as a gift. The Prophet ﷺ ate some of the dates this time.

That was the second sign! Salman told himself. He bent over, searching for the seal of prophethood on the Prophet's back. Prophet Muhammad ﷺ knew what he was looking for, so he took off his garment and showed his back to Salman. That confirmed that this was the Messenger of Allah ﷺ. Prophet Muhammad ﷺ had fulfilled all three signs of prophethood. Salman threw himself on the Messenger of Allah ﷺ, hugging him, and embraced Islam on the spot.

From then on, Salman loved spending time with the Prophet ﷺ. However, he was still a slave, and his master would not allow him to participate in any of the events with the other Muslims.

Prophet Muhammad ﷺ cared about his companions and wanted to help Salman. He advised Salman to ask his master to set him free. His master agreed, but said he had to plant one hundred date palm seeds and wait for them to grow into trees if he wanted to be free. That would take more than fifteen years!

Prophet Muhammad ﷺ asked his companions to help their brother in Islam. They all worked together to prepare the land and dig holes for planting the date palms. Prophet Muhammad ﷺ placed every seed in the ground and made *dua* for Salman to be set free quickly. With the blessings of the Prophet ﷺ and the will of Allah ﷻ, the seeds grew into palm trees within three years. Salman was set free!

Prophet Muhammad ﷺ worked together with his companions to free Salman from slavery. They demonstrated the power of teamwork and cooperation in achieving a goal.

The Battle of the Trench

Prophet Muhammad ﷺ received news that the Quraysh and other Arab tribes had created a large army and were planning to attack the Muslims in Medina.

Prophet Muhammad ﷺ held a meeting with his companions and shared the Quraysh's plot. The Muslims did not have enough time to prepare an army and leave Medina. They had to find a way to stay and protect the city from the attack. They brainstormed together for a solution, and Prophet Muhammad ﷺ carefully listened to everyone's opinion and thought about each option.

Salman al-Farisi had a brilliant idea. He said, "In Persia, whenever we hear an attack is coming, we dig a huge **trench** around the entire city to protect it." Prophet Muhammad ﷺ, who was always open to new ideas, loved this suggestion. He held a vote, and everyone agreed that it was the best solution. This was the first time in the Arabian Peninsula that this method was used to protect a city.

Since they only had about two weeks to dig the huge trench, Prophet Muhammad ﷺ gathered all the companions and started digging right away. Prophet Muhammad ﷺ was an older man now, but he supported his companions and helped them dig the trench. They did not have **advanced tools**, but through collaboration and teamwork, the trench was ready in time for the attack.

The trench was the perfect surprise. Their enemies had never seen anything like it before, and they didn't know what to do. They tried to cross it, but the trench was too wide. They were unable to reach Medina. They eventually lost the battle and had to return to Mecca.

Even though the Muslims faced a lot of challenges, their hard work and cooperation helped them dig the giant trench and save Medina. Prophet Muhammad ﷺ and his companions demonstrated the power of teamwork.

Why couldn't the enemies cross the trench?

Practical Application Questions

- Think of a time when you worked with a teammate on a project. How did it make you feel? Why do you think teamwork matters?
- List ways having good character qualities, like those of the Prophet ﷺ, can improve teamwork.
- Describe the characteristics you can see in a good team member.

18. Leadership

What Is Leadership?

Leadership means being a guide for those around you and helping others work together toward a goal. A leader isn't someone who just tells people what to do; instead, they inspire people by being hard-working, understanding, and kind. A good leader can create a vision of the future and share that dream with others. You can become a leader by developing important skills like confidence and empathy. First you need to believe in yourself and then make sure everyone on your team feels included and motivated to do their best!

How Did the Prophet ﷺ Practice Leadership?

- Prophet Muhammad ﷺ believed in himself and his ability to spread the message of Islam. He had a clear vision and always motivated others to work toward that goal.
- Prophet Muhammad ﷺ was a role model for others. He taught by being a good example and doing the right thing.
- He ﷺ never gave up when faced with challenges. He stayed positive because he knew that Allah ﷻ loved him and cared for him.
- He ﷺ always had a positive attitude and the desire to succeed.
- He ﷺ understood the strengths of others and used their strengths to build a unified team. This allowed them to work together in the best way to achieve a goal.

Leadership in Action

The Treaty of al-Fudul

Prophet Muhammad ﷺ was involved in his society from a young age. He was raised in the houses of the great leaders of Mecca, which prepared him to be a leader. Before becoming a prophet, he always defended human rights, like justice and safety. He supported the oppressed and took care of orphans and widows. He was known for his compassion and love for his community—he never hesitated to help.

When Prophet Muhammad ﷺ was twenty-five years old, an incident occurred in Mecca. A rich man from the Quraysh owed money to a poor salesman from Yemen, but the rich man refused to give the salesman what he owed. Without that payment, the salesman had no money to get back home to Yemen. When the leaders of Mecca heard about this incident, they held a meeting to write a **treaty** (or an agreement).

Prophet Muhammad ﷺ was invited to attend this meeting because he was seen as a future leader. The Prophet ﷺ told us about this treaty: "They all agreed to support the rights of whoever was oppressed." The leaders of Mecca decided to support the weak, regardless of their background or the tribe they came from.

This was a very unusual decision; Arabs living at the time of the Prophet ﷺ respected people based on their tribe. It was not common to protect people who were poor or powerless. This important treaty was known as *Hilf al-Fudul* (**the Treaty of al-Fudul**).

Prophet Muhammad ﷺ was involved in his community, supporting justice and participating in the important decisions of his society. By the time he became a prophet, his noble character and love of his community were already well-known. Prophet Muhammad ﷺ cared about everyone in the city and led the way to protecting the oppressed and fighting for justice. Thirty years later, when he established the Constitution of Medina, he drew inspiration from the important Treaty of al-Fudul.

Why do you think Prophet Muhammad ﷺ was seen as a future leader, even before he became a prophet?

The Boulder and the Prophecy

Our beloved Prophet ﷺ was granted many miracles from Allah ﷻ. Among his miracles were several predictions (or prophecies), where he accurately foretold events that would happen in the future.

When the Muslims were preparing for the Battle of the Trench, they dug a trench around the city of Medina to protect it from attack. All of the Muslims participated in the digging, including the Prophet ﷺ.

One day, the companions could not dig any farther because they had reached a huge boulder. Every time they tried to hit it, the ax would break instead of the boulder! They asked the Prophet ﷺ to help them find a solution. The trench had to be ready quickly—before the city was attacked by Quraysh. They had to break through the boulder, and they had no time to waste.

Prophet Muhammad ﷺ took an ax and headed to the boulder. As he struck the boulder, he said: "Bismillah! Allahu akbar! I have been given the keys of **Sham**! I can see its red palaces." Then he struck the boulder again and said: "Allahu akbar! I have been given the keys of Persia. I can see **al-Mada'in's** white palace." When he struck the boulder for the third time, he said: "Allahu akbar! I have been given the keys of Yemen. By Allah ﷻ, I can see the gates of Sana'a." The boulder fell to pieces, and the Muslims were able to keep digging the trench to protect the city of Medina.

Prophet Muhammad ﷺ led by being available to help his team solve problems. And in this case, he was given a vision from Allah ﷻ that Islam would spread to these lands (Sham, Persia, and Yemen). He shared that **prophecy** with his companions, and this helped them prepare to continue spreading the message of Islam, even after the Prophet passed away.

The Story of the *Adhan*

Prophet Muhammad  was a great leader who respected his companions, listened to their opinions, and discussed ideas with them. Whenever the Prophet ﷺ met with his companions, he would listen to their suggestions and ask their opinions before he made any decisions.

When the Muslims first moved to Medina, they all worked together to build the new masjid so they could perform **salah** (prayer) together.

At first, people were confused about when to pray—they weren't sure when the prayer times began. Prophet Muhammad ﷺ, who was an exceptional problem solver, decided to hold a meeting with his companions and brainstorm some ways to call people to prayer.

Some companions suggested using a bell, while others suggested using a horn, but Prophet Muhammad ﷺ was not in favor of either idea. They continued suggesting ideas, but nothing sounded right to the Prophet ﷺ. The meeting ended and they all went back home, still trying to think of a good solution.

One of the companions at the meeting was Abdullah ibn Zayd. He was thinking about this issue all night, until he finally fell asleep. That night, he had a dream in which he went to purchase some items—a horn and a bell—to call for salah.

Then a person in his dream asked him, "Should I not tell you of something better than that?"

"What?" said Abdullah (*radi Allahu anhu*).

"When you want to call for prayer, say:

اَللَّهُ اَكْبَرُ - اَللَّهُ اَكْبَرُ

اَللَّهُ اَكْبَرُ - اَللَّهُ اَكْبَرُ

اَشْهَدُ اَنْ لَا اِلٰهَ اِلَّا اللهُ - اَشْهَدُ اَنْ لَا اِلٰهَ اِلَّا اللهُ

اَشْهَدُ اَنَّ مُحَمَّدًا رَسُولُ اللهِ - اَشْهَدُ اَنَّ مُحَمَّدًا رَسُولُ اللهِ

حَيَّ عَلَى الصَّلَاةِ - حَيَّ عَلَى الصَّلَاةِ

حَيَّ عَلَى الْفَلَاحِ - حَيَّ عَلَى الْفَلَاحِ

اَللَّهُ اَكْبَرُ - اَللَّهُ اَكْبَرُ

لَا اِلٰهَ اِلَّا اللهُ

Allahu akbar, Allahu akbar.
Allahu akbar, Allahu akbar.
Ashhadu an la ilaha illallah.
Ashhadu an la ilaha illallah.
Ashhadu anna Muhammadan Rasulullah.
Ashhadu anna Muhammadan Rasulullah.
Hayya ala al-salah. Hayya ala al-salah.
Hayya ala al-falah. Hayya ala al-falah.
Allahu akbar, Allahu akbar.
La ilaha illallah."

Allah is the Greatest! Allah is the Greatest!
Allah is the Greatest! Allah is the Greatest!
I bear witness that there is no god except Allah.
I bear witness that there is no god except Allah.
I bear witness that Muhammad is the Messenger of Allah.
I bear witness that Muhammad is the Messenger of Allah.
Hurry to the prayer. Hurry to the prayer.
Hurry to success. Hurry to success.
Allah is the Greatest! Allah is the Greatest!
There is none worthy of worship except Allah.

As soon as Abdullah woke up, he went straight to the Prophet ﷺ and told him about his dream. Prophet Muhammad ﷺ confirmed that this was a vision from Allah ﷻ. He immediately called for Bilal ibn Rabah (*radi Allahu anhu*) and said: "Stand up, oh Bilal, because you have the best voice." He asked Abdullah ibn Zayd to teach Bilal the words of the *adhan*. Bilal recited the words and with that, Bilal became the first muezzin in Islam.

Explain how Prophet Muhammad ﷺ demonstrated good leadership skills in "The Story of the *Adhan*."

Practical Application Questions

- Think of a time when you believed in yourself and chose to be a leader. What happened? How did it make you feel?
- List ways you can show leadership in your everyday life.
- Describe the characteristics you can see in a good leader.

19. Kindness

What Is Kindness?

Kindness means being friendly and considerate to others. A kind person is nice and does good deeds without expecting anything in return. Being a kind person means caring for others and forgiving them when they make mistakes—even when it's hard to do. Kindness means sharing love with those around us and acting with compassion.

How Did the Prophet ﷺ Practice Kindness in His Life?

- Prophet Muhammad ﷺ showed kindness in the best of ways to everyone around him.
- He ﷺ always shared stories of kindness with his companions to teach them the importance of this characteristic. He taught us to greet others with a kind word and reply with a better one.
- Prophet Muhammad ﷺ was known for his beautiful smile. He encouraged others to smile as often as they could, and said this was a form of charity—meaning that we are rewarded by Allah ﷻ when we smile at someone!
- He ﷺ always tried to help others physically, emotionally, and financially.
- Everyone around him ﷺ felt treasured by his love because of his compliments and kind words.
- Even though he ﷺ had a lot of responsibilities, he would always go out of his way to support others.
- He ﷺ would shake hands with everyone and was always the last one to let go.
- Prophet Muhammad ﷺ forgave others when they treated him badly and even showed love toward them.

Next time you're shaking hands with someone, remember the Prophet ﷺ, and do not let go until they do. Try to notice how the other person felt and think about how you felt too! Then send *salawat* upon the Prophet ﷺ.

Kindness in Action

The Prophet's Promise

Jabir (*radi Allahu anhu*) accepted Islam as a young boy in Medina. His father, Abdullah ibn Hiram (*radi Allahu anhu*), was a great companion of the Prophet ﷺ. He passed away and left behind seven young daughters. Jabir found himself in charge of his sisters and was their only provider.

When the Muslims were coming back from the Battle of Dhat al-Riqa', Jabir was riding an old camel and was lagging behind the rest of the army. He didn't have enough money to buy a strong, fast camel.

Jabir was sad and worrying about how he would provide for his sisters when he was barely making any money.

Then he heard a voice calling his name. "Jabir!" He looked up and it was Prophet Muhammad ﷺ approaching him with a beautiful smile on his face.

Usually the leaders rode in front of the army, but Prophet Muhammad ﷺ had come to the back to check on Jabir. Even though the Prophet ﷺ had many responsibilities and was in charge of the whole army, he was able to show kindness to everyone around him.

Prophet Muhammad ﷺ asked Jabir why he was sad. "Because my father passed away, leaving me seven sisters to take care of."

Prophet Muhammad ﷺ tried to make him feel better by asking about his family and wife. When the Prophet ﷺ noticed how slow Jabir's camel was, he asked him to stop. Prophet Muhammad ﷺ put his hand on Jabir's camel and said: "Bismillah!" Suddenly the camel became much faster. The camel became so fast that Jabir was now riding in front of the army. This was one of the Prophet's miracles.

Prophet Muhammad ﷺ continued to stay close to Jabir and asked if he would sell him his camel. He asked how much Jabir wanted for the camel and joked that maybe he would sell it for one dirham.

"No, this is a fast camel now!" Jabir replied to the Prophet's joke.

"I will buy it for forty dirhams. I will pay you once we arrive in Medina." Prophet Muhammad ﷺ said. Jabir was overjoyed, because his camel was the only thing he owned, and he was happy to receive such a large amount of money for it to help support his sisters.

When they arrived in Medina, Prophet Muhammad ﷺ was welcomed by many people and was busy talking to them. Jabir did not bother the Prophet ﷺ or interrupt him. He simply tied his camel next to the Prophet's door as a reminder of his promise.

When the Prophet ﷺ saw the camel, he smiled and called Jabir. He paid him the forty dirhams and said: "I will also gift you the camel." Jabir was truly happy and thanked the Prophet ﷺ for his kindness. Prophet Muhammad ﷺ wanted to give money to Jabir from the very beginning, but he did not want him to feel embarrassed that he was receiving **sadaqa** (charity) from him.

A Noble Brother

Years after the migration to Medina, the Muslims signed a treaty with the people of Mecca to ensure that peace was kept between them. Prophet Muhammad ﷺ honored the treaty, but the people of Mecca soon broke it. When the Prophet ﷺ learned about this **violation**, he gathered his army and ten thousand Muslims marched toward Mecca. When they entered the city, no one dared stand against their huge army. Allah ﷻ had blessed the Prophet ﷺ with victory after all the hardships that he and the Muslims had endured.

Everyone watched and waited to see what the Prophet ﷺ would do to the people of Mecca, who had tried to kill him and his companions. Prophet Muhammad ﷺ entered the city humbly and thanked Allah ﷻ for His blessings. He recited **Surat al-Fath** while he walked straight to the Kaaba.

19. KINDNESS

$$\text{لَقَدْ صَدَقَ ٱللَّهُ رَسُولَهُ ٱلرُّءْيَا بِٱلْحَقِّ لَتَدْخُلُنَّ ٱلْمَسْجِدَ ٱلْحَرَامَ}$$
$$\text{إِن شَآءَ ٱللَّهُ ءَامِنِينَ مُحَلِّقِينَ رُءُوسَكُمْ وَمُقَصِّرِينَ لَا تَخَافُونَ}$$
$$\text{فَعَلِمَ مَا لَمْ تَعْلَمُوا۟ فَجَعَلَ مِن دُونِ ذَٰلِكَ فَتْحًا قَرِيبًا}$$

God has truly fulfilled His Messenger's vision: "God willing, you will most certainly enter the Sacred Mosque in safety, shaven headed or with cropped hair, without fear!"—God knew what you did not—and He has granted you a speedy triumph. Quran 48:27

He pulled down the idols and began to make **tawaf**—the rite of Hajj where the pilgrims circle the Kaaba. He then entered the Kaaba with Zayd and Bilal (*radi Allahu anhuma*) and prayed inside. The Prophet ﷺ walked out, stood in front of the people of Mecca, and said "*La ilaha illallahu wahdahu la sharika lah.*" (There is no god but Allah alone, and He has no partner.)

The Prophet ﷺ asked Bilal to call the *adhan* from the top of the Kaaba. Bilal, who was once tortured by the leaders of Mecca, was now standing on the Kaaba calling the *adhan*.

Then Prophet Muhammad ﷺ looked at the people of Quraysh and asked them: "What do you think I am going to do with you?"

They said: "Only good—you are a noble brother and the son of a noble brother."

Prophet Muhammad ﷺ replied to them with the same thing Prophet Yusuf (Joseph) (*alayhi al-salam*) said to his brothers:

$$\text{قَالَ لَا تَثْرِيبَ عَلَيْكُمُ ٱلْيَوْمَ يَغْفِرُ ٱللَّهُ لَكُمْ وَهُوَ أَرْحَمُ ٱلرَّٰحِمِينَ}$$

There is no blame on you today. May Allah forgive you! He is the Most Merciful of the merciful! Quran 12:92

Prophet Muhammad ﷺ embodied kindness in the best of ways. Even when he had the opportunity to get **revenge** on the people who had hurt him and his followers for years, he chose to be kind and forgive them for everything they had done.

Why do you think Prophet Muhammad ﷺ chose to respond to the disbelievers in Mecca the same way Prophet Yusuf responded to his brothers in Egypt? How do you think the people of Mecca felt when they heard the Prophet ﷺ say those words?

A Mercy to Humankind

Prophet Muhammad ﷺ was the noblest of people and the kindest in heart. His compassion and kindness showed in his beautiful smile, bright face, and gentle words, and captured the hearts of everyone around him. The companions loved to be in his presence. They gathered around him at al-Masjid al-Nabawi to recite the Quran, remember Allah ﷻ, and learn from the Prophet's wisdom. The masjid was a sacred place. It was always kept clean and tidy, symbolizing respect and devotion.

One day, a Bedouin entered the masjid as the Prophet ﷺ was sitting there with his companions. He was not from Medina and was unaware of the etiquette of the masjid. He looked around and, to everyone's surprise, he began to urinate right there inside the masjid.

The companions were shocked. They jumped up to stop the man and scold him, but the Prophet ﷺ gently raised his hand and told them, "Do not stop him, let him finish." The companions were shocked but knew there was wisdom behind Prophet Muhammad's actions. They stepped back, leaving the man alone.

When the Bedouin was done, Prophet Muhammad ﷺ called him over with a kind smile on his face. He did not scold him; instead, he explained to him the customs and etiquette of the masjid by gently saying: "These masjids are not suitable for any kind of urine or filth. Instead, they are places for the remembrance of Allah, prayer, and the recitation of the Quran."

The Bedouin realized he had made a mistake and felt embarrassed by his action, but the Prophet ﷺ spoke to him with kindness and understanding.

The Prophet ﷺ asked one of the companions to bring a bucket of water. He taught the companions how to purify the area from urine by pouring a bucket of water on it and cleaning it thoroughly.

The Prophet's kindness toward the Bedouin amazed everyone in the masjid. They learned a valuable lesson that day that stayed with them forever, and they shared this story with others, spreading the Prophet's teachings of compassion and wisdom.

Practical Application Questions

- Think of a time when you showed kindness even though you could have been harsh. What did you do? How did it make you feel?
- List ways you can show kindness to others.
- Describe the characteristics you can see in a kind person.

20. Respect

What Is Respect?

Respect means treating others the way you would like to be treated. When we respect someone, we care about their feelings. We understand how our words and actions affect them. You can show respect to someone by speaking kindly, listening, and being polite. Respect means understanding that everyone deserves to be treated with the same level of fairness and consideration, no matter who they are.

How Did the Prophet ﷺ Practice Respect?

- Prophet Muhammad ﷺ treated everyone around him with kindness and respect.
- He always valued people's opinions, especially his companions, whom he always sought advice from.
- He ﷺ accepted others for who they were; it did not matter where they came from or how they looked.
- The Prophet ﷺ was a good listener; he did not interrupt people, and he responded in a way that showed he cared.
- He ﷺ was considerate of everyone around him and understood their needs and rights.
- When Prophet Muhammad ﷺ spoke to someone, he would turn his whole body to completely face the person he was speaking to.
- When the Prophet ﷺ spoke, he was sensitive to others' feelings. He never used harsh words.

Respect in Action

The Keys to the Kaaba

Years after leaving Mecca and settling in Medina, Prophet Muhammad ﷺ and his companions gained victory in Mecca and were able to enter the city again. This was known as the Liberation of Mecca or *Fath Makka*. Prophet Muhammad ﷺ then became the new leader. He and his companions entered al-Masjid al-Haram happily, while saying *takbir* ("Allahu akbar"). Prophet Muhammad ﷺ approached the Black Stone, then made *tawaf,* walking around, or **circumambulating,** the Kaaba seven times.

At that time, 360 idols were lined up around the Kaaba. All of them were destroyed and removed, and the space around the Kaaba was cleared. Prophet Muhammad ﷺ prayed two *raka'as* of prayer, then went to the Well of **Zamzam** to drink and make **wudu** (ritual washing before prayer). He climbed the hill of al-Safa, made *dua,* and thanked Allah ﷻ for this blessing.

After making his *dua*, he wanted to enter the Kaaba, but the door was locked. He asked Uthman ibn Talha (*radi Allahu anhu*), whose family held the key to the Kaaba, to bring it for him. Uthman brought it from his house and gave it to the Prophet ﷺ. Prophet Muhammad ﷺ opened the Kaaba door and entered with Bilal, Usama ibn Zayd, and Uthman ibn Talha (*radi Allahu anhum*). Prophet Muhammad ﷺ prayed two *raka'as* and made *dua*.

Uthman ibn Talha thought that the Prophet ﷺ would keep the key himself now. Instead, he locked the Kaaba and gave the key back to Uthman. This was an enormous show of respect for Uthman's family, who had held the honor of overseeing the Kaaba's key for years. Prophet Muhammad ﷺ announced that this key should remain with Uthman's family, and no one should take it away from them. His family holds the key to the Kaaba to this day because Prophet Muhammad ﷺ respected their rights and treated them with fairness and dignity.

The Humble Host

When Prophet Muhammad ﷺ arrived safely in Medina, he stayed in Abu Ayyub al-Ansari's house while his own was being built. Abu Ayyub and his wife (*radi Allahu anhuma*) were honored to host the Prophet ﷺ. Their house had two floors, and he wanted the Prophet ﷺ to stay on the second floor, believing it would be more comfortable for him.

Prophet Muhammad ﷺ showed respect for Abu Ayyub's privacy by asking to stay on the first level of the home. Prophet Muhammad ﷺ was expecting many guests to visit him, and he didn't want to bother Abu Ayyub and his family with all of those visitors. Abu Ayyub agreed to stay on the second floor of the house. He wanted Prophet Muhammad ﷺ to be comfortable and happy. For each meal, Abu Ayyub and his wife sent food for the Prophet ﷺ to eat. They would not eat before he did, due to their utmost respect for him.

One day, while Abu Ayyub and his wife were upstairs, water accidentally spilled on the floor. They were so worried that water would leak through the floor and drip onto Prophet Muhammad ﷺ that they spent the whole night cleaning it up.

Abu Ayyub loved the Prophet ﷺ and respected him greatly. He went downstairs and insisted that the Prophet ﷺ move to the second floor. When the Prophet ﷺ told him that he still preferred to stay on the first floor (to respect Abu Ayyub's privacy), Abu Ayyub said, "Oh Messenger of Allah ﷺ, how can we live on top of you? It is not respectful to have the feet of Abu Ayyub walk on top of the head of the Prophet ﷺ." Eventually the Prophet ﷺ agreed to stay on the second floor so as not to distress Abu Ayyub and his wife.

Abu Ayyub loved and respected the Prophet ﷺ, and Prophet Muhammad ﷺ showed Abu Ayyub the same kindness and respect.

Legs as Heavy as a Mountain

Abdullah ibn Mas'ud was the sixth person to embrace Islam. He had many great qualities, and one of them was that he was very humble. He was also the keeper of the Prophet's secrets.

Abdullah was very close to the Prophet ﷺ and narrated hundreds of hadiths. He also had a great knowledge of the Quran.

Once, Prophet Muhammad ﷺ was gathered with some companions and asked Abdullah to climb a tree and pick some dates for them to eat. As he climbed, the companions saw his shins and noticed how skinny they were. This made them laugh.

When the Prophet ﷺ noticed them laughing, he said: "What are you laughing at? The legs of Abdullah? By the One who has my soul in His Hand, the two of them [his two legs] are heavier in the balance than Uhud [a large mountain in Medina]."

The Prophet ﷺ told the companions that Abdullah's legs were more valuable to Allah ﷻ, and had earned more good deeds on his scale, than the weight of a mountain. Prophet Muhammad ﷺ taught the companions to treat everyone with respect, regardless of how they look.

Practical Application Questions

- Think of a time when someone treated you disrespectfully. What happened? How did it make you feel?
- List ways that being respectful can help the community.
- Describe characteristics you can see in a respectful person.

21. Gratitude

What Is Gratitude?

Gratitude means noticing and appreciating the blessings in our lives. We can be grateful to Allah ﷻ when we are thankful for everything He has given us. A grateful person notices the good things in their life, appreciates them, and acts upon this feeling by saying "**alhamdulillah**" (all thanks and praise be to God) and by doing good deeds.

How Did the Prophet ﷺ Practice Gratitude?

- Prophet Muhammad ﷺ was grateful to Allah ﷻ and everyone around him.
- Whenever someone helped him, he ﷺ would thank them.
- He ﷺ always liked helping those around him and found ways to serve the community.
- The Prophet ﷺ was able to focus on positive things even when he was in a difficult situation.

Gratitude in Action

Loyalty

When the Muslims returned to Mecca, Prophet Muhammad ﷺ and the Muhajirun (**emigrants** from Mecca to Medina) were happy to enter their beloved city once again. It had been many years since they were forced to leave it and migrate to Medina. Now they were able to pray freely around the Kaaba, and their hearts were full.

The Ansar, the people of Medina who first welcomed Prophet Muhammad ﷺ to their land, were happy for the Prophet ﷺ and the Muhajirun, but they were also worried that the Prophet ﷺ would leave them and move back to Mecca. They loved the Prophet ﷺ dearly and didn't want to be left behind.

Prophet Muhammad ﷺ respected and loved the Ansar. They had welcomed him in Medina when his people tried to kill him. They even welcomed all the Muhajirun, sharing their houses, wealth, and money. When they were attacked by the people of Quraysh, they fought side-by-side with the Prophet ﷺ and protected him. He ﷺ was grateful for all they had done for him and the Muslims.

Angel Jibril (*alayhi al-salam*) informed the Prophet ﷺ about the worries of the Ansar. Curious to hear their answer, Prophet Muhammad ﷺ asked the Ansar if they were upset. They said, "Yes. We are afraid that you will leave Medina and live in Mecca."

Prophet Muhammad ﷺ expressed his gratitude to the Ansar and assured them that he would remain living in Medina and would always be one of them. He told them that their blood was his blood and their life was his life.

Prophet Muhammad's kind words touched their hearts.

The Grateful Servant

Prophet Muhammad ﷺ was always grateful to Allah ﷻ for His blessings. He expressed his gratitude through worship. He would spend days in the cave of Hira worshipping Allah ﷻ to show his thankfulness for the blessings he had. Aisha (*radi Allahu anha*), Prophet Muhammad's wife, narrated that when the last ten days of Ramadan began, Prophet Muhammad ﷺ would spend most of his nights worshipping Allah ﷻ.

She noticed that the Prophet ﷺ would stand in prayer for hours, even though his feet became swollen and began to hurt. She wondered why he spent so much time worshipping when his sins had already been forgiven. He had already been promised Janna! So she asked, "Oh Prophet of Allah, why do you pray so much when Allah ﷻ has forgiven all your mistakes already?"

The Prophet ﷺ responded: "Shouldn't I be a grateful servant?"

Prophet Muhammad ﷺ worshipped Allah ﷻ to show his gratitude for all of Allah's blessings. He was grateful that Allah ﷻ had forgiven him and granted him Janna.

21. GRATITUDE

Honoring Khadija

Khadija (*radi Allahu anha*) was Prophet Muhammad's first wife. She supported him in every possible way. When Angel Jibril (*alayhi al-salam*) visited the Prophet ﷺ for the first time, he felt scared and confused. He went to Khadija trembling and shaking. She covered him, assured him with her kind words, and reminded him that Allah would never disgrace him with visions that weren't true. She became the first person to believe in the Prophet's message and the first person to embrace Islam.

When the Prophet ﷺ declared the message of Islam and people tried to hurt him, Khadija used her wealth to hire guards for him. The guards protected him from the people of Mecca who wanted to stop him from spreading the message of Islam. Khadija always used her wealth to support the Prophet ﷺ.

She used her money to buy food secretly for the Muslims during the boycott, when the Quraysh did not allow them to buy any food. Prophet Muhammad ﷺ was always grateful to his wife, and he loved her dearly for all that she had done for him and for the Muslims. When she passed away, he was very sad. The year she died is called the Year of Sorrow.

Years later, Prophet Muhammad ﷺ was out walking and recognized some of Khadija's friends from far away. He immediately took off his robe and spread it on the ground for them to sit on. He was very welcoming to them and very generous. One of the companions asked the Prophet ﷺ why he was treating them so kindly and with so much respect. Prophet Muhammad ﷺ said they were Khadija's friends, and he was expressing his gratitude to Khadija by treating her friends well.

Some time later, Prophet Muhammad ﷺ saw a necklace of Khadija's, and tears trickled down his blessed cheeks. When his companions asked him why he was crying, he told them how grateful he was for all the support she had given him and the rest of the Muslims.

How did Khadija show her gratitude toward Prophet Muhammad ﷺ? How did Prophet Muhammad ﷺ show his gratitude toward Khadija?

> **Practical Application Questions**
> - Think of a time when you helped someone and they showed gratitude to you. What happened? How did that make you feel?
> - List ways you can show gratitude to others.
> - Describe the characteristics you can see in a grateful person.

Mabrūk! Congratulations! **Mashallah**! Now that you've finished *My Prophet, Myself*, let's have some fun reflecting on the lessons you've learned from the Prophet ﷺ.

Which character traits do you feel are your strengths? Write down your top three along with an example of how you show each trait in your life. Say "Alhamdulillah!"

What are three character traits you wish you could be better at? Think of three traits you want to strengthen and come up with one idea to practice each trait in your life.

Finally, let's talk about our favorite stories from Prophet Muhammad ﷺ, his family, and his companions. Share your favorite story, why you liked it, and one lesson you learned from it!

Final Reflections

Our thoughts can influence our feelings, and our feelings can influence our actions. The way you think about yourself and your life can make a huge difference in your happiness. When we think positive thoughts, we will want to do positive things. Focus on the blessings and strengths Allah ﷻ has already given you. Remember that your challenges in life are a chance to become stronger and grow closer to Allah ﷻ. When you believe in yourself, you will be able to turn difficulties into opportunities. Remember that making mistakes and learning lessons are part of growing up.

We tend to think that our happiness comes from what *happens* to us, but the reality is that happiness comes from *how we respond* to what happens to us. The path to happiness is like a map, and we get to choose how to follow it.

Choosing to make a change in yourself by adopting the character traits of Prophet Muhammad ﷺ will give you the strength and confidence to stay positive no matter what challenges you face.

Believe in yourself—you are capable of amazing things!

Rabbana taqabbal minna innaka anta al-Sami' al-Alim.
Our Lord, accept [this] from us. Indeed You are
the Hearing, the Knowing. Quran 2:127

Glossary

English

accuse: To charge someone with a fault or offense

advanced tool: A sophisticated instrument or device used to accomplish a task

appearance: The way someone or something looks

astonish: To surprise or amaze someone greatly

attendee: A person who attends an event

boycott: Refusing to engage in trade or social relations with a person, group, or country in order to protest their actions

brink: The edge or point at which something is about to happen

caravan: A group of people, especially traders, traveling together across a desert in Asia or North Africa

characteristic: A trait or quality that is typical of a person or thing

circumambulate: To walk around something, often referring to walking around the Kaaba during pilgrimage

commander: A person in authority, especially in the military

companion: A follower of Prophet Muhammad ﷺ who met and supported him during his life

compassion: Concern for the suffering or misfortunes of others

confess: To admit or acknowledge something, especially a wrongdoing

considerate: Thoughtful of others; showing regard for the feelings or needs of others

constitution: A set of fundamental principles or established precedents governing a state or organization

coping mechanism: A technique or method used to deal with stress or a difficult situation

criticize: To express disapproval of someone or something

cruel: Describes a person or an act that causes pain or suffering to others

deceive: To trick or mislead someone

dignity: The honor or respect that each human should give themselves and others

dispute: An argument or debate

dozens: Large numbers; usually referring to multiples of twelve

eager: Wanting to do or have something very much

embodied: To represent or symbolize something in a tangible form

emigrant: A person who leaves their country to live in another

empowered: Having the power or authority to do something

event: Something that happens, especially something important

exaggerate: To represent something as larger or more important than it really is

exclude: To deny someone access to or participation in something

expansion: The action of becoming larger or more extensive

expel: To force someone to leave a place

fame: The state of being well-known or recognized by many people

fasting: Abstaining from food, drink, and other specific physical needs for a set period of time, especially during Ramadan

filth: Unclean matter, often used metaphorically to describe moral or spiritual corruption

foster parent: A person who cares for a child that is not their own by birth

genealogy: The study of a person's family and ancestors

harsh: Unpleasantly rough or severe

Hebrew: The Semitic language historically spoken by the Jewish people

hesitation: The action of pausing before saying or doing something, especially due to uncertainty

humble: Not thinking of oneself as better than others

idols: Statues or images that people worship as gods

insist: To demand something forcefully, not accepting refusal

investigate: To carry out a systematic or formal inquiry to discover and examine facts

Judaism: The monotheistic religion of the Jewish people, based on the teachings of the Torah

lineage: Direct descent from an ancestor; pedigree

luxurious: Extremely comfortable, elegant, or enjoyable, often expensive

morals: Standards of behavior or beliefs about what is right and wrong

mule: An animal the size of a horse, with the longer ears of a donkey

noblewomen: Women of high social rank or birth

opposition: Resistance or dissent, expressed in action or argument

oppress: To treat someone cruelly or unjustly

persecute: To treat someone unfairly or harm them because of their beliefs or identity

pilgrimage: A religious journey, often referring to Hajj

possessions: Things that are owned

predict: To state or estimate that something will happen in the future

preserve: To keep safe; protect

profit: A financial gain or benefit

profit: To get some good out of something; gain

prophecy: A prediction of future events, especially one that is divinely inspired

prostration: Bowing down during Islamic prayer

Quraysh: The dominant tribe in Mecca during the time of Prophet Muhammad ﷺ, many of whom opposed his message

rank: A position within a hierarchy

rejection: The act of being refused

revenge: The act of retaliating for a wrong or injury

righteousness: The quality of being morally right or justifiable

seal of prophethood: A physical mark on the back of Prophet Muhammad ﷺ symbolizing his role as the final prophet

shelter: A place giving protection from bad weather or danger

sincere: Free from pretension or deceit; genuine

tactic: An action or strategy carefully planned to achieve a specific goal

temptation: The state of strongly wanting to do something one considers to be wrong

thorns: Sharp points on plants that can hurt people or animals

throne: Refers to the throne of Allah (ﷻ) in an Islamic context, often mentioned in relation to divine power

treaty: A formal agreement between parties or groups, often countries or tribes

trench: A defensive ditch dug around Medina to protect the city during the Battle of the Trench

trendy: Very fashionable or up-to-date

unbearable: Not able to be endured or tolerated

violation: The act of breaking or disregarding rules or agreements

widow: A woman whose husband has died

Arabic

ﷻ: A phrase meaning "May He [Allah] be glorified"

ﷺ: A phrase meaning "Peace and blessings be upon him [the Prophet Muhammad]"

adab (أدب): Islamic manners, etiquette, or moral conduct

adhan (أذان): The Islamic call to prayer, recited five times a day

al-amanat (الأمانات): Trusts; items or responsibilities entrusted to someone

alhamdulillah (الحمد لله): A phrase meaning "All praise is due to Allah"

al-Mada'in (المدائن): The historical capital city of the Persian Empire, near modern-day Baghdad

al-Masjid al-Nabawi (المسجد النبوي): The mosque of the Prophet Muhammad ﷺ in Medina, the second holiest site in Islam

al-Najashi (النجاشي): The title of the Christian king of Abyssinia (Ethiopia) who sheltered Muslims during the early days of Islam

al-nughayr (النغير): A type of sparrow, referenced in a story

al-Sadiq, al-Amin (الصادق الأمين): Titles of Prophet Muhammad meaning "the Honest, the Trustworthy"

al-Suffa (الصفّة): A sheltered platform behind the Prophet's mosque in Medina where the poor and homeless among the Muhajirun lived

alayhi al-salam (عليه السلام): A phrase meaning "Peace be upon him," used when mentioning the prophets and angels

Allah (الله): The Arabic word for God

ashhadu an la ilaha illallah wa ashhadu anna Muhammadan rasulullah (أشهد أن لا إله إلا الله و أشهد أن محمداً رسول الله): The declaration of faith in Islam, meaning "I bear witness that there is no god except Allah, and I bear witness that Muhammad is the Messenger of Allah"

assalamu alaikum (السَّلَامُ عَلَيْكُمْ): A greeting meaning "Peace be upon you"

astaghfirullah (أستغفر الله): A phrase meaning "I seek forgiveness from Allah" *aya* (آية): A verse from the Quran

bismillah (بِسْمِ اللهِ): A phrase meaning "In the name of Allah;" used before beginning something

bismika Allahumma (باسمك اللهم): A phrase meaning "In Your name, oh Allah"

Dhul Hijja (ذو الحجة): The twelfth and final month of the Islamic lunar calendar, during which the Hajj occurs

dua (دعاء): A prayer

Fajr (فجر): The early morning prayer in Islam

fiqh (فقه): The rules for how to live as a Muslim, like how to pray, what to eat, or how to behave; Islamic jurisprudence

hadith (حديث): A report or saying of Prophet Muhammad ﷺ

Hajj (حج): The Islamic pilgrimage to Mecca

hijra (هجرة): The migration of Prophet Muhammad ﷺ and his followers from Mecca to Medina

huffaz (حفّاظ): People who have memorized the entire Quran

Janna (جنة): Paradise or Heaven

Jibril (جبريل عليه السلام): The angel Gabriel, who delivered messages and revelation from Allah to the prophets

Kaaba (الكعبة): The sacred building in Mecca

khutbah (خطبة): A talk given during a religious service; lecture, talk

la ilaha illallah (لا إله إلا الله): The first part of the Islamic declaration of faith, meaning "There is no god except Allah"

masjid (مسجد): Mosque, a place of worship for Muslims

mashallah (ما شاء الله): A phrase meaning "What Allah has willed"

minbar (منبر): A pulpit in the mosque from which the imam delivers sermons

Muhajir, Muhajirun (مهاجر مهاجرون): The Muslims who migrated from Mecca to Medina

muezzin (مؤذن): The person who calls Muslims to prayer

Prophet Muhammad (النبي محمد): The last prophet of Islam *radi Allahu anhu/anha/anhuma/anhum* (رضي الله عنه/عنها/عنهما/عنهم): A phrase meaning "May Allah be pleased with him/her/them both/them"

raka'a (ركعة): A unit or cycle of prayer in Islam

sadaqa (صدقة): Charity or voluntary giving in Islam

salah (صلاة): The formal prayers in Islam, performed five times daily

shahada (الشهادة): The Islamic declaration of faith

Sham (الشام): Refers to the historical region encompassing modern-day Syria, Lebanon, Palestine, and Jordan

sujud (سجود): The act of placing one's forehead on the ground during Islamic prayer

sunna (سُنَّة): The practices of Prophet Muhammad ﷺ

Surat al-Fath (سورة الفتح): Chapter 48 in the Quran, titled "The Victory"

Surat al-Rahman (سورة الرحمن): Chapter 55 in the Quran, titled "The Most Compassionate"

Surat Maryam (سورة مريم): Chapter 19 of the Quran, named after Maryam (Mary) the mother of Jesus

tawaf (طواف): The act of walking around the Kaaba

Treaty of al-Fudul (حلف الفضول): An agreement made in Mecca to support the rights of the oppressed

Thawr (غار ثور): The cave where Prophet Muhammad ﷺ and Abu Bakr (*radi Allahu anhu*) hid during the migration to Medina

ummah (أمة): The global Muslim community

yaqeen (يقين): Certainty or conviction, especially in the context of faith in Allah's plan

zakat (زكاة): An obligatory form of charity in Islam

Zamzam (زمزم): A sacred well in Mecca

Bibliography

Al Habbal, Wassim Saad El Deen and Zeina Ahmad Jaroudi Sanyoura. *Revive Your Heart with 52 Prophetic Ethics.* Kalima Ṭayyiba, 2022.

Al-Bajuri, Muhammad al-Khudari Bak. *The History of the Four Caliphs.* Turath Publishing, 2012.

Al-Zāyid, Samīra. *Mukhtaṣar al-jāmiʿ fī al-sīra al-nabawiyya.* N.p., 1995.

Hashimi, Talib. *Women of Excellence in the Time of the Prophet.* Turath Publishing, 2022.

Tabaa', Asma. *Stars in the Prophet's Orbit.* Self-published, 2003.

"The Califh Uthman Bin Affan Endowment." Awqaf. https://www.awqaf.gov.sa/en/endowment-example/endowment-Othman-well.

Index

A

Abdullah ibn Abi Rabia 59
Abdullah ibn Mas'ud 43, 112
Abdullah ibn Zayd 77, 99, 100
Abdul Muttalib 36, 42, 84
Abu Ayyub al-Ansari 110
Abu Hurayra 76
Abu Jahl 42, 43, 59, 64
Abu Lahab 36, 37, 39, 40, 58, 59, 68
Abu Lubaba 47
Abu Talib 17, 36, 37, 38, 65, 66, 67, 84, 85
Abu Umayr 6
adhan 77, 78, 100, 105, 122
Aisha 28, 66, 76, 114
al-Abbas 39
al-Aqsa Mosque 78
al-Arqam ibn Abi al-Arqam 26
al-Hasan 22
al-Husayn 22
Ali ibn Abi Talib 13, 22, 33, 47, 84
al-Mada'in 97, 122
al-Masjid al-Haram 110
al-Masjid al-Nabawi 55, 75, 89, 90, 106, 122
al-Najashi 32, 59, 60, 122
al-Safa 26, 110
al-Suffa 75, 76, 77, 122
Amina 84
Amr ibn al-As 59, 60, 81
Anas ibn Malik 6, 85
Asma 75, 125

B

Banu Abd Manaf 11
Banu Hashim 65
Battle of Badr 27, 39, 47
Battle of Dhat al-Riqa 102
Battle of the Trench 92, 97, 121
Battle of Uhud 44, 81
Battle of Yamama 33
Bilal 52
Bi'r Uthman 55
boycott 37, 38, 65, 66, 67, 115, 118

C

Constitution of Medina 48, 96

D

Dar al-Arqam 23, 27, 42
Dhul Hijja 58, 123

F

Fatima bint Asad 84, 85

H

Hajj 17, 46, 58, 74, 75, 86
Hamza ibn Abdul Muttalib 42
Haritha 45, 46, 67
Hilf al-Fudul 96
Hira 29, 32, 114

K

Kaaba 11, 23, 26, 40, 42, 43, 44, 64, 65, 66, 78, 104, 105, 110, 113, 118, 123, 124

Khalid ibn al-Walid 81
Khunnas 23

L
Liberation of Mecca 110

M
Maysara 10
Medina 4, 6, 13, 24, 27, 28, 30, 48, 53, 59, 61, 70, 71, 72, 74, 75, 77, 78, 79, 80, 86, 89, 90, 91, 92, 93, 94, 96, 97, 98, 102, 103, 104, 106, 110, 112, 113, 114, 121, 122, 123, 124
Mus'ab ibn Umayr 23
Mut'im ibn Adi 37, 39

N
Nusayba bint Ka'ab 44

O
offer to the Prophet 17

P
Persia 72, 91, 94, 97
Pledge of al-Aqaba 73, 75
prophecies 97

Q
Quraysh 13, 17, 26, 32, 37, 38, 41, 42, 52, 58, 59, 64, 65, 66, 67, 69, 70, 92, 93, 96, 97, 105, 114, 115, 121

R
Ruqayya 32

S
Safiyya 36

Sa'id ibn al-As 33
Salman al-Farisi 91, 94
Sana'a 97
Suhayb al-Rumi 63, 69
Suraqa ibn Malik 71, 72
Syria 10, 124, 128

T
Ta'if 66, 67, 68
Thawr 61, 124

U
Umar ibn Abi Salama 22
Umar ibn al-Khattab 33, 41, 43, 77, 78, 86
Umayya ibn Khalaf 52
Urwa ibn al-Zubayr 28
Uthman ibn Affan 32, 33, 53, 55
Uthman ibn Talha 110
Uthman's Well 53
Uways al-Qarani 86

V
Valley of Abu Talib 38, 65

W
Waraqa ibn Nawfal 30

Y
Yemen 10, 33, 45, 86, 96, 97

Z
Zamzam 110, 124
Zayd ibn Haritha 45, 67
Zayd ibn Thabit 25, 33

About the Author

Dana Nass integrates character building into every curriculum she designs and every class she teaches. *My Prophet ﷺ, Myself* is her first foray into the world of engaging textbooks for young people.

Holding a master's degree in psychology and behavioral analysis from Grand Canyon University, Nass currently serves her community as a behavior specialist and youth leader. She studied traditional Islamic subjects with renowned scholars in Damascus, Syria, as well as through Rabata, earning *ijazas in* Hafs recitation of the Quran and the Forty Hadith of Imam Nawawī.

Residing in Arizona, Dana finds joy in life's simple moments—savoring a cup of coffee or spending time with her family.

www.ingramcontent.com/pod-product-compliance
Lightning Source LLC
Chambersburg PA
CBHW061120070526
44583CB00028B/3346